ENTER FATIMA

or

what happened when customs officers discovered body parts in my suitcase

Charlotte York

United Kingdom, www.dentdeleone.com — written by Charlotte York, illustrations by Betsy Bickle, photography unless otherwise stated åbäke, edited by Jonathan P. Watts, cover by LPPL, designed by åbäke, printed by Aldgate Press in London; ISBN: 978-1-907908-79-8 Thank you Luna Suzuki Ståhl, Damo Suzuki, Kajsa Ståhl, Loraine Furter, Jean-Baptiste Levée, Bardhi Haliti, Anna Colin, Lydia Lee, Léonore Emond, Anne Millet, Khalil Rabah, Tirdad Zolghadr, Yaïr Barelli, Noura Al Khasawneh, Nick Booth, Lisa Mazza, Mone Mair, Gemma Holt, Sandra Doublet, Ian Lynam, Tania & Chantal Garduño, Benjamin Reichen, Joëlle Le Saux, Amanda Crabtree, Francesco Finizio, Emmanuelle Queau, Boris Achour, Margaux Robilliard, Ninon Martin, Léa Mainguy, Inès Miossec, Antonia Carrara, Nina Krawczyk, Aurélien Froment, Alexis Bouillon, Ignacio Guzman, Mélusyne Faucard, Manu Luksh, Ilona Roux, Post Poetics in Seoul, Ruth Sibbille, Sébastien Deltombe, Manual Reader, Killian Ryan, Suky, Matteo Delahaye, Johanna Schäffer, Rob Sollis, Ryoji Suzuki, Emmanuelle Queau, Sébastien Noel, Charlotte Mainguet, Patrick Lacey, Jesper Ståhl, Mahala Guillaume, Hugo & Cat Kostrzewa Duverger, Ricardo Rodríguez Elías, Martino Gamper, Mukul Patel, Eva Rucki, Jochen Dehn, Francis Upritchard, Jean-Claude Chianale, Angela Richier, Utrecht in Tokyo, Benjamin Patti Smith, Hussein Chalayan, Milly Patrzalek, Prune & Matteo Chianale Poux, Elsa Poux, Ève Chabi, Margarita Del Rio, Harry Thaler, Laura Pappa, Per Hüttner, Sara Vaz, Marco Balesteros, Matthieu Becker, Jan Steinbach, Fabien Cappello, Vincent Humeau, Eline McGeorge, Dan Eatock, Sofie Dederen, Yuki Matsuzaki, Sean Yendrys, Boris Charmatz, Jackie Chan, Yoko Ono, Steve Aoki, Bun Hay Mean, Oh Dae-su, Ai Wei Wei, Michael Ashley Fowler, Rita Davis, Gréta Þorkelsdóttir, Mark Foss, Oliver Long, Dave Grohl, Patrick Zavadskis, Aleksandrs Brickže, Raïssa Kim, Ophélie Summer, Damien Marchal, Maud LePladec, Frank Philippin, Quentin Schmerber, Paula Buškevica, Björn Giesecke, Otso Peräsaari, Alejandro Bellón Ample, Louise Borinski and Marianne Hultman

contents

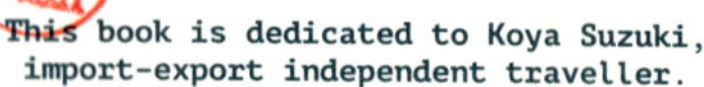

This book is dedicated to Koya Suzuki,
import-export independent traveller.

Me? In a quarter-full lecture theatre, a man is seated at a desk, on the left of the stage a laptop, a microphone, an apple and a glass of water in front of him. He uses the laptop as a hiding place as people arrive later than the time advertised for the lecture.

He is painfully reminded of friends showing up late and looking sorry they missed what was clearly announced. He is saddened that they assume they know his work so well they can't be bothered to give some benefit to any doubt. They would perhaps be surprised; they'd see he tries hard to challenge his own preconditioned behaviour.

After a while he stands up, takes a bite in the apple to which he previously glued a leaf, grabs the microphone and says: "Dear reader, what follows is a talk given in front of live audiences. It was mostly given in English, parfois en Français and, once, *nihongo de shaberimashita*." He places the apple back on the table, hoping at least one person notices the similarity to the Apple company logo.

The speaker looks at the audience and smiles nervously:

"What precedes may seem at odds with the fact this is a talk and I seem to be addressing someone else who is reading what is happening right now, in a book. This person is located in our future although if I say 'hello reader', this is in her/his present."

The speaker chuckles, embarrassed.

"An artist talk such as this one aims at introducing someone's practice and I am assuming you came to see some Art and design projects or if you are reading this you found the book in a specialised bookshop full of publications one can't quite find in wider distribution outlets."

"You see me standing in front of you but in reality I am in my pyjamas, typing those very words at approximately 6am in a dark October morning, planning both a future talk in which I'll be more or less reading this and a further future of a book in which this will be printed."
Now, I am typing this.
Now, you are hearing it.
Now, you are reading it.

[The back of the stage lights up and reveals a dining table for a dozen people. A woman sits on the right and a man on the left, the smell of food one could have noticed when entering the lecture theatre now makes sense but further awakens the empty stomachs of some members of the audience.

The woman, named Greta, stands up, executes a gracious cartwheel, ever so slightly loses balance but only to catch her left shoe and use it as a microphone. She quietly sings for a minute, her gaze locked towards the audience. With an accent you recognise as Icelandic she says:"Hey! Welcome".]

[The man, named Michael, stands up and is given the shoe. He is thin and tall, his make-up highlights his eyes, also locked towards the audience. His long arms move around his face in a voguing fashion, his nose ring catches the projector lights and with an accent you recognise as Canadian he says: "When the speaker of this lecture, who is a member of a collective of four, is requested a short biography he obliges with the following options of standard maximum character/word count he has often been asked to respect."]

Maximum 300 characters:
åbäke is a group of four people working from Copenhagen, London and Stockholm since 2000. A primary source of inspiration for our works would be context, an encounter,

a place or a constraint such as providing a bio of no more than 300 characters, even if it means that it can get suddenly interrupte

Maximum 50 words:
Fifty words to fairly define twenty years of activities is a truly challenging affair. Solicited or not short self-written biographies predate selfies but somehow follow similar rules of editing a version of oneself until we start to look very attractive indeed. We would start by saying that åbäke is a

Between 50 to 70 words.
Fifty to 70 words to fairly define 16 years of activities of a collective is truly challenging. Short biographies predate the selfie but somehow follow similar rules of editing a version of oneself until we start to look very attractive indeed. We would start by saying that åbäke is a
Or rather and for once, we propose a different perspective on the biography which perhaps will raise questions, mainly on

9

[Michael passes the microphone shoe to
the speaker
who looks like this,
according to
his 9-year-old
daughter.]

"Thank you,
I have a friend
called Ryan
who is a professional artist.
In his line of work there are many
occasions to thank people, in exhibitions,
publications, public talks etc. He is really
good at thanking people and seems to never
quite forget anyone, which is both a good
skill to master but also the basic courtesy
of acknowledging one can't do everything

alone. Thanking people induces stress. A sense of injustice can cloud the exercise. Some people did help a lot, others less, some with a heart or an ear, others with money. You thank people who didn't know they helped and don't thank others who adamantly believe they did. These populations cross the ones who want to see you thank them and the others who don't. Is it better being forgotten than forgetting?

Our collective used to work for fashion designer Hussein Chalayan and for his retrospective exhibition at the Design Museum in London. We designed all the graphics, paper, digital and the exhibition displays with the interior architects. A serious amount of work and lots of exciting meetings with Hussein. He'd be quite unique in pacing the room, suddenly sitting on the floor, the physical manifestation of a brain in a storm, too busy to think for other functions of the body. It was exhausting but thrilling to come up with ideas with him on the spot. We had a blast and felt a good connection. Then came the exhibition private view which we enjoyed. A week later, we received a bunch of T -shirts from Hussein's studio and we were very happy for this unexpected gift. We immediately called Milly, his assistant, to thank her since her name was on the card. She was very apologetic and told us she had completely forgotten to invite us to the private view dinner and the presents were a small gesture etc. She sounded very nervous. We were a little hurt but those dinners are usually very stiff so we just shrugged it off as a mistake that happens. To this day I still wear the T -shirts.

This talk is about visual identity and since it is also a book the reader will miss what is evident to you, the audience: the way the speaker looks, his, my, visual identity.

According to my then five-year-old daughter, this is how I looked:

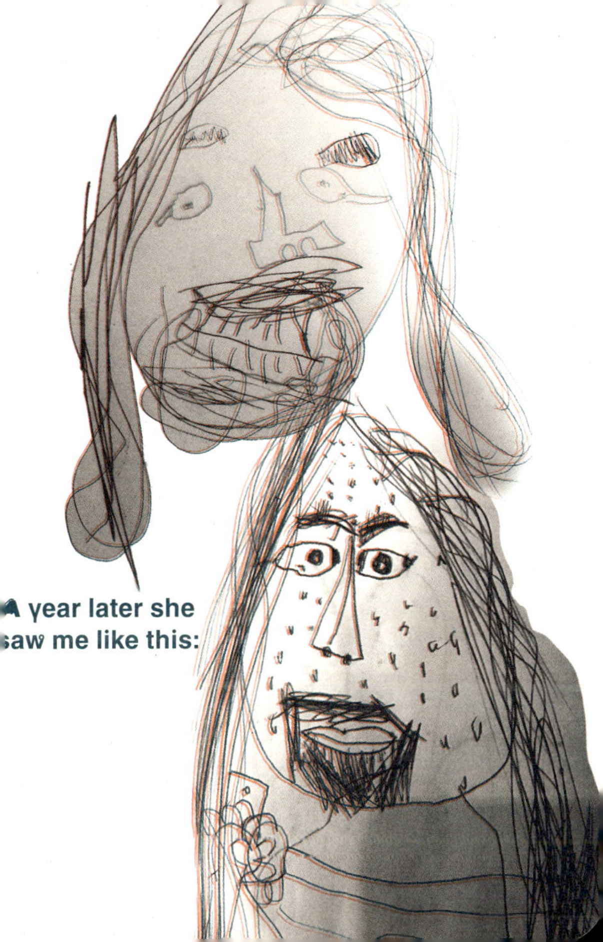
A year later she
saw me like this:

What information can you gather from the way people look? Their visual identity doesn't necessarily convey who they really are but it is certainly difficult to avoid first impressions. Today I look this way: I chose these clothes but it is because I washed my hair and bought new apparel. It was my assumption none of you knew me so I tried with this shirt that, if you ask my friends, is out of character and frankly uncomfortable but for you, you might think I just have eccentric taste and you could congratulate yourself for being open minded. We once asked students to come dressed in an embarrassing outfit they owned for a group photo at the beginning of a workshop. They bravely wore what they considered shameful but if I didn't tell you about it, would you notice?

The visual identity is what we want to project. It is not necessarily who we really are. It might be who we think we are, more often than not a better version.

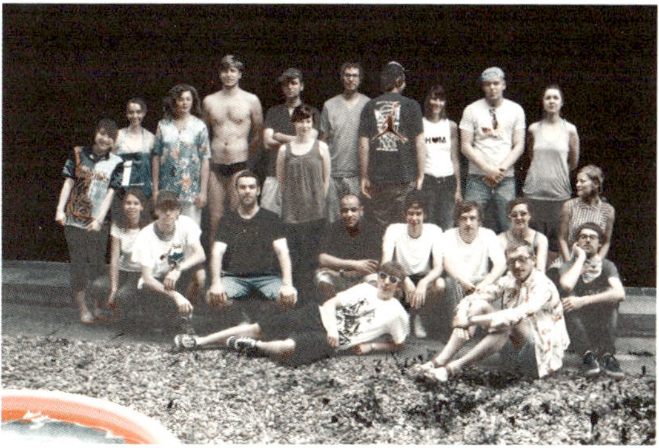

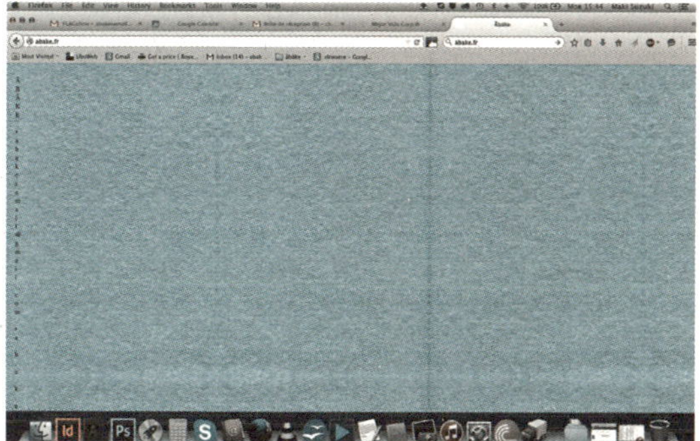

Below is our website, a single page.

An anonymous commentator enquired whether it was on purpose that this is not only useless, but also ugly. Such blunt honesty created a moment of doubt and I was taken aback, equally offended but somehow proud.

I wondered about their taste in general, passing judgement at their judgement or credentials. Can I take his comment as a compliment or do I reconsider my own sense of aesthetics?

What did this person mean by ugliness? Are we ugly? If we go back to the function of a website and how it represents you, this minimal website felt correct at the time. On the other hand, this never was part of a grander scheme and strategy of deep beliefs through appearances as we were just very busy making things and not having time representing them... None of us in the collective wanted to work on the website. It didn't help that one of us described it as "reheating leftovers in a smelly microwave and garnishing it with a leaf of plastic parsley". Why did we even have a single page on the net is another relevant question. The simpler and radical solution could have been to avoid any website at all. One could invoke the old cliché of the cobbler who wears the worst shoes. A shoe that seemed offensively ugly in addition to the frustration of a portal leading nowhere as this first page was also the last, an immediate dead end. Another graphic design friend with an extensive and quasi-exhaustive website asked if it was a criticism of people like her, making everything available online.

We said no.

When I was vegetarian, I constantly had to answer aggressive questions from omnivorous French until I realised they didn't care so much about what my choice meant to me but rather focused on what my choice meant for them. If I am vegetarian and I say it, am I attacking non vegetarians? If I have long hair, will you take it as a comment on your short hair?

When I go to a party, an opening of an exhibition or some other such social gathering, there is always someone, usually a man, in the corner of the room whose presence I can feel, the way you know or sense being observed. In my peripheral vision this man is smiling and looking for eye contact. Statistically he could be a friend so I concede and engage eye contact. He is a complete stranger who understands this eye contact as a permission to come aboard. He will suddenly appear next to me with an excessive smile and will say, "Hey, where are you from?" without much more of an introduction.
I'll say, "Well, I'm from London."
And he'll say, "Yeah, but originally?"
So, I'll say, "Well, I am French,
                      I was born in France."
And then this man will insist, "Yeah, but originally?"
And then I will have to say, "Well, my parents are Japanese."
And then he will say, "Aaah!" with the

satisfaction of someone who's known this all along. My guess is he walked across the room for validation. Most of them would conclude this non exchange by saying something in Japanese in what I can only assume is their subtle way to verbally wink at the fact they love Japanese culture. I never really know what to say about this, because I am of Japanese ancestry, but I feel trapped by my visual identity. Am I trying to convey the complexity of where one comes from despite this face as visual identity? The conversation with these guys never really goes anywhere. I doubt it is motivated by actual curiosity. Once he gets my "confession" he usually goes back to his corner. This is a rather bland encounter but at least it seems harmless. In comparison, there is another kind, equally frequent, a little bit scary, with men from across the street or in a passing car with the window open who shout, "Hey, Jackie Chan!" It is a very common occurrence and it has happened in Europe, in the Middle east, Africa or the Americas, not so much in Asia. This is how famous this guy is. I don't look at them but I am always flattered. Jackie Chan is very famous for doing his own stunts in action movies and if I translate this in terms of being a designer, what's often missing is that we tell someone else's story, someone else's work. In other words we don't do our own stunts. When I get called Jackie Chan, I hear the cheers. "Jackie Chan, very good! You can do it too!"

I wonder why I don't get called Bruce Lee.
I posed this question to my friend Pierre.
He shot a deadpan look: "It's because you
don't look like Bruce Lee at all."

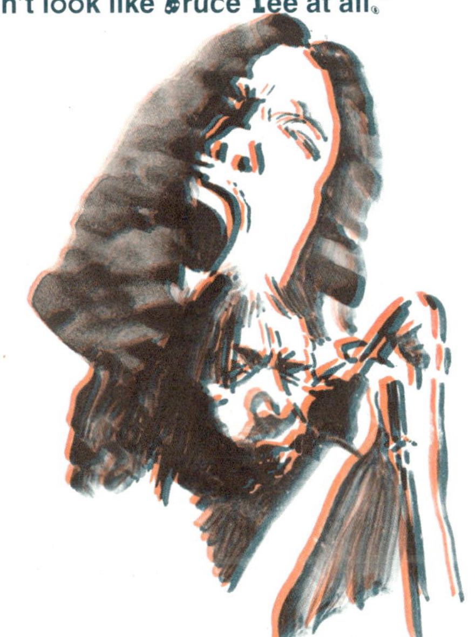

"Hey Damo! Damo Suzuki!" I turn around.
Inevitably, this is in a bar.

Damo Suzuki was part of the legendary krautrock band Can in the seventies. So, when people ask, "Hey, aren't you Damo Suzuki?", I answer "If you think that I was in my twenties in the seventies, then yes,

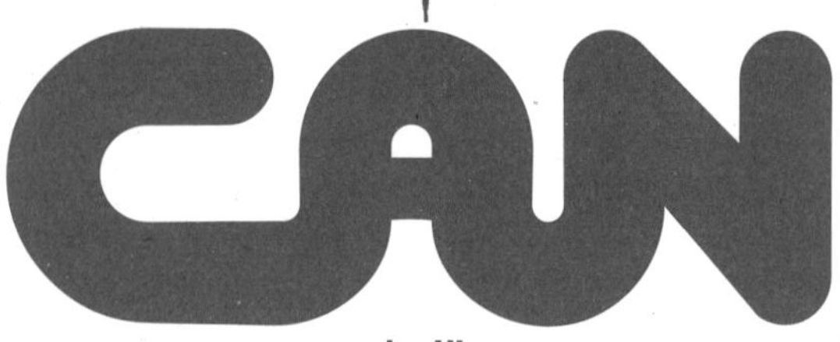

be!" I mostly say yes because I like the band. I once got a free drink because the bartender said, leaning towards me in this very noisy and dark place, "Damo, thanks mate, this beer's on me." I took the pint, smiled and thanked him back. This time warp is exciting: a cool young bartender in 2019 can believe I was in an experimental rock band in 1970. I am a fraud, a rock star for a day. More often than not, I get called Damo by people who are older. It is very rare for a millennial to call me Damo. One of his strong qualities is longevity. I met him in his late sixties. He tours non stop and improvises for hours with local bands. He's continuously been singing live for more than half a century, in and out of fringe fashion. Music is cruelly young, made by and consumed by young people. Damo transcends the deadlines of fashion, he is longevity and perseverance.

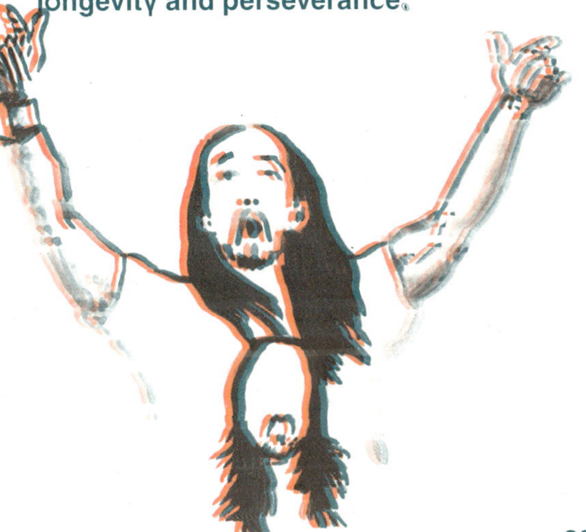

I walk past some high school students in France and I hear "Stevie!", I am on a bus in the Netherlands and I hear a group of boys shout "Stevie!" The people who call me that are almost always teenagers. They probably don't know Damo Suzuki even if music genres don't create specific tribes anymore. Steve Aoki is a popular DJ. I know of him because I was called Steve Aoki so many times I looked it up. I hear, "Oy, Stevie!" I turn around, wink and finger gun with a broad smile.

I hang out in a Belgian club with a friend who looks like Pedro Winter, another celebrity from that world. Two frauds getting attention. I make people happy about it by nodding or signing autographs although they don't quite question that a superstar DJ would probably not be on a bus but what do I know? I once sat in the London underground and, oh surprise, Mike Leigh was in front of me. For sure, a left-wing British film director is not the same as an American mainstream DJ but they perhaps

share the use of public transport because
of principles or even taste.

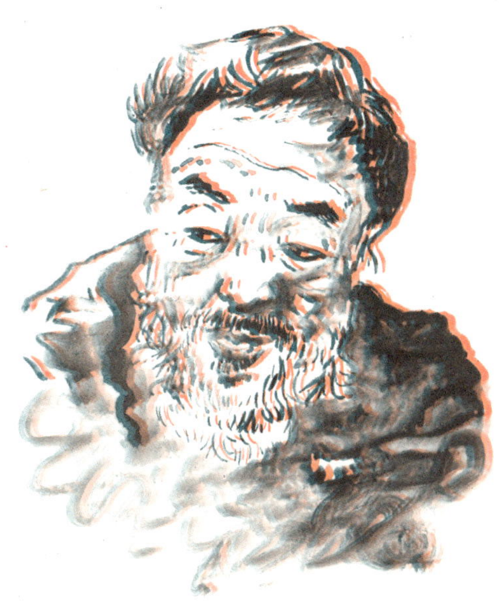

A man in an electric wheelchair came to
me in a park and started chatting about the
weather, how spring had sprung. I was with

an artist friend and although this guy was rather friendly we noticed he didn't speak to both of us but only to me. I initially thought he was intimidated by women, especially with blue hair as Manu adorned that day. The conversation became more specific about Art and I tried to include Manu but the man continued to ignore her. He had a very strong opinion about a big installation of millions of fake sunflower seeds by Chinese artist Ai Wei Wei in the Turbine Hall of Tate Modern some years ago. He had been there in the early days of the show and pocketed loads of the fake seeds like most people as in the beginning it wasn't exactly clear whether this was allowed or not. Manu interjected she did too but the man persevered in ignoring her. By the time I went to see it, a week or two after the opening, it was fenced off and the invigilators were instructed to keep people away from stealing.

The conversation was interesting despite the awkward exclusion of Manu by this guy. At some point he stopped talking and, looking at me, he frowned and suddenly said: "Wait, you're not Ai Wei Wei!"

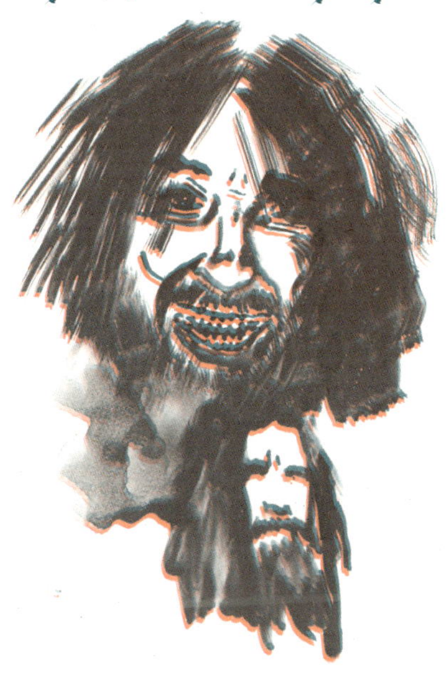

People yell "Oldboy" at me. Even when I was younger. They don't call me "old boy" but "Oldboy", who is a character in a neo-noir movie by Park Chan-wook, he's not a real person. The film is very violent but mind blowing. It is a story of revenge, redemption, reminiscent of Japanese folk tales, manga and arguably the leading film in the early 2000s Korean wave cinema. Oldboy is a mediocre guy who is kidnapped for 15 years, kept in a cell without windows. He doesn't know why he is held captive and watches the world go by on his TV and the rest of the movie unfolds as a complex set of characters, reasons, plots in which almost nobody's innocent etc. When people call me Oldboy they mean I am a complex person. I don't have to be perfect. I have stolen things. I have sometimes been cruel to people, disingenuous, lied even. But, I'm only human and when I am called "Oldboy", I think of calling my mum to tell her I love her and not only because I am scared of being kidnapped and kept in a cell for 15 years. I can change.

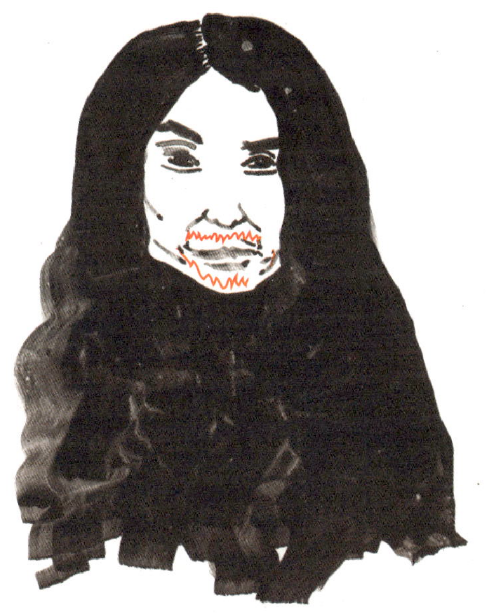

In the corner of my eye I see a man waving his phone, pointing at it. He is all smiles, peacocking. As I turn around he cannot help show the disgust of realising I am not the woman he intended to get the phone number of.

I'm called Yoko Ono, by guys who don't see gender. I like her work. Especially a black and white film of moving buttocks and her book *Grapefruit*, instructional proposals for artworks. I also love grapefruit.

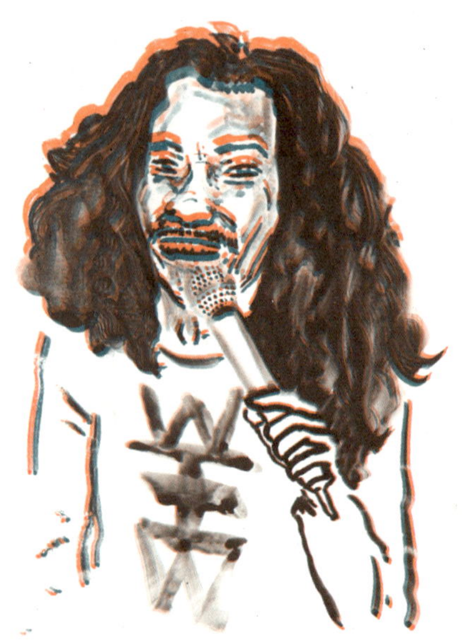

Sitting at the terrace of a café on a sunny day, Yaïr and I order an espresso and a glass of water. This is the south of France and we expect the conventional grumpy waiter to behave as reluctantly as possible. Instead, the white-shirted rotund man holding an empty tray immediately comes to us not only without showing contempt but with a genuine looking smile, a rare event. I am convinced of the underground training camp for café garçons where happy youngsters are turned into middle-aged grumpy men, an obligatory attitude within the profession. We order the minimum, which is an espresso and tap water. It will dampen his illogical mood, we think, but no, he locks eye contact, even, and his smile, contrary to the wildest prognostics, widens. What is going on? "Good morning gentlemen," he says. I notice he ignores Yaïr, almost as if after having shown the required politeness to both he'd chosen to speak to me only. Come to think of it, he did have a frowned face when we clocked the terrace from the opposite pavement but became all smiles when he saw us. "My daughter is a big, big fan," he adds, after taking our order. I swear he punctuated this with a wink. "You won't mind me asking for an autograph," he almost commands, albeit with a slightly uncomfortable subservient tone. As I look around at the other waiters, it is clear he is the boss and doesn't usually serve clients. He came for me. But which me? He disappears to get the coffees and a notepad. Yaïr looks at me dumbfounded. I had told him about such possibilities but I only now realise he didn't believe me. Most of my friends don't know this happens. The boss comes back, whistling a tune, skipping to a happy tune in his head. His face is very close to mine: "Her name is Jenyfer. She will be SOOO happy." I smile, take his pen and pad, write with bold letters "Jenyfer, good luck for all your projects and personal thank yous," followed by a scribble that fills the rest of the page. I make sure it has an average number of illegible characters for it to become whatever name one has in mind. He takes the pad, reads the message, tries to decipher the signature, possibly thinks there are too many letters but concludes it is legit. One more thank you, maybe a bow and he shakes my hand, having forgotten I am with someone else. Yaïr is looking at me, stunned. I follow the boss entering his café and showing the autograph to his employees who all look at me. I hide a little and we quickly finish our espresso. Yaïr knows better than to ask me who they thought I was.

Ben Gurion

My plane from Istanbul landed in Ben Gurion airport in Tel Aviv; my final destination: Ramallah. When the event I am about to tell happened, Palestine was not equipped with an international airport. Given the existing tensions between Israel and Palestine, I had been warned to be extra careful at the customs. Most of my travels were motivated by curiosity and financed by a project: a workshop, a residency, a lecture, a design assignment etc. I was actively trying to develop a practice which would allow travel and therefore require physical presence.

Queuing to show my passport, I observe the three lines and fall into preconceptions I'd point a judgemental finger at. On the left, a possibly Swedish, most definitely blonde, girl with a "kärnkraft, Nej Tack" T-shirt with long dreadlocks and expensive-looking bohemian clothes was showing confidence. On the right, a family of five, possibly Ethiopian, fumbled nervously through printed documents while a soldier studied them from the aisle. Just behind them, an south Asian man with long hair trails a Rimowa luggage covered with stickers. This man could be me. In the middle, six well-trimmed generic men between 30 and 60 years old are standing neatly behind each other. I choose to queue behind them. They are more than in the lateral lines, but unfortunately, I guessed right, and it goes faster. The funnel of law is sometimes painfully predictable. It only slows down when I hand in my passport and the customs officer verifies what's on the document and the reality. I glance to my left and right; the dreadlocks girl and the family are still stuck answering questions. I have learned to smile and present myself as willing to cooperate, especially since I do not have much to hide.

The custom officer sits in a cubicle, protected with bulletproof glass and must be sitting on a platform unless he is a giant. Whatever my height, he'd look down on me. I hadn't done anything wrong and immediately wondered why I thought this. Faced with authority, I constantly scan my memory for the possible reasons I am being questioned. I start feeling guilty and reason my way back to concluding I am innocent. I could think of a special outfit and hairstyle for going through customs. We have been in the XXIst Century for more than a decade, but long hair for men still seems more suspicious than short. Have they not read what Pasolini wrote about this? Since the sixties, it is no longer a dissident gesture but, at best, just being lazy and, at worst, being a poseur. I just want to go through the customs fast.

My skin colour is on the lighter end of the spectrum. Being short, I suppose, has the advantage of seeming to be less threatening in case a physical interaction might occur, but perhaps my Asian face cast doubt on hidden skills of Martial Art.

The Customs officer asks: "Have you ever been to Africa?" And I have to think hard because the situation is, you know, you blank the memories entirely in moments someone with authority – and a gun, I am imagining – asks you a question like this.

The obvious answer is the truth, and it would have to be a yes, but wait, is there a reason he specifically chose the continent? Why not South America or Antarctica? Other thoughts come flashing of customs officers in the States, quizzing on how many times and from each airport one has landed in the USA. Sweating, trying to recall the year and if vicious, they'd ask the month, looking at the screen where the answers are. Me, naive, thinking that if you know, why ask me? I am me, I swear.

Have I been to Africa?

It took me a while to say "yes, I have." "I've been to Morocco," I zealously add, satisfied to answer positively, suddenly standing in front of a teacher.

The custom officer rolled his eyes. I firmly believe that someone with so much power is not allowed to do this. A doctor, for example, should never be allowed to roll their eyes, teachers, police etc.

In this tennis match the ball came back too fast on my court. Wrong answer? Another attempt? What did I say which was so bad? Custom officer, slightly annoyed tells me: "I said Africa."

Maybe I got my geography wrong, but I added, "I also have been to Tunisia," satisfied. And he rolls his eyes again. Slightly angry this time, he repeats with a sigh, "Africa," the shortening of his words clearly indicates his patience level is diminishing. I get it; there was something subjective about geography. Taiwan is a country to me, not to China. In this context and time, when an ebola crisis was occurring, Africa was short for Western African countries. So, I guess it's not entirely his fault that he didn't listen in school about geography.

The Sphinx had a second question. I felt my body heat and decided against removing my jacket as it could be interpreted as a hostile gesture. The less I move, the more I smile. Make myself smaller, slowly narrow my shoulder.

"Have you ever been to the Middle East?" Yes, yes, I have. Slamming the buzzer, stop the countdown; I have the answer! I have been to Jordan a few times… – I was trying to be jovial, casual even. I look at him, my head slightly tilted like a puppy waiting for appraisal. I wagged my tail.
He rolled his eyes and said: "Apart from Jordan?" in a tone of disappointment and not quite believing how moronic I was. My knowledge of the region is basic, but I was aware that having traveled to Syria, Lebanon or Egypt through Israeli customs could have raised eyebrows. But I had not. And despite historical complications, Jordan and Israel were okay with each other. In a way, it was the only place I could have been, and I was giving myself ten points. He looked disappointed. No more geography discussions, then.

Friends had warned me that if the Israeli authorities stamped my passport, it would make it that much more complicated to travel to some countries such as Lebanon or Syria, both very high on my wish list. I also dreaded the question of my final destination as I didn't feel at ease lying to a custom officer. He didn't ask nor stamp my document. Overall, very easy to get through to Palestine.

I got my luggage and went to do my job; I met the people, the curators, and the architects. On the second day of this trip, I was offered to visit a village near Jerusalem, and we crammed into a taxi. Quite serious architects, serious curators and I, trying to keep up with the whole thing, we were a little overwhelmed by the elephant in the taxi. Every conversation, wherever they started, was clouded by the political situation but each and everyone present was making an effort. The ambience in the car was good-humoured, cheerful even, with some architectural jokes on my right and a little Art gossip on my left. As we were getting closer to a checkpoint, the important and serious cultural ambassadors and workers I was with were visibly nervous. The concrete watch tower was getting closer. Not so tall but the tallest in the landscape of rare trees and low hills. We could not see if anyone was watching behind the reflecting windows, but we knew someone was looking at our car, driving slowly toward them. Three military jeeps were parked. Reaching the tower, I saw… three teenagers. From a distance, they could be 16. This is visual identity from afar; I look at them and think, yeah, they are 15, 16, maximum 17. Two… I was going to say boys, ok, two men, one woman. Their fresh faces were surrounded by adult equipment, helmets, camouflage uniforms, pockets everywhere, impeccable high boots and with massive guns. It could have been comical, as if some weird parents had dressed their kids in military regalia. The seriousness of the situation, however, was indicated to me by the change of attitude in the taxi. Everyone was silent, looking straight ahead, somehow submissive. Why were those successful middle-aged mid-career designers, artists, and curators so afraid of three kids? A puzzling, not altogether uninteresting power imbalance.

Our taxi stops. One soldier gets closer to the window; he commands us to wind it down. Everyone avoids eye contact except me as I notice he is intensely looking. I'm intensely looking at him in defiance, except my gaze shifts downwards from his eyes to the side of his nose, where a giant mole is hypnotising me. This doesn't seem right and I force my eyes to go back up but inevitably and ashamedly, they slide down again and again towards the mole, a most fascinating feature in an otherwise perfect face. The mole is not ugly; it just takes so much space and horizontal latitude my mind wanders off on whether he constantly sees the mole in his peripheral vision. Is the mole making him self-conscious? I hope he doesn't notice my distraction.

Do people mention his mole all the time? If not verbally but from the gaze? Similar to a grain of rice on a cheek, a salad leaf on a tooth distracts the person you are talking to constantly while they cannot signal the source of their distraction. I try to focus on the severe eyes, the scrutiny this military boy exercises and the fear he instills. Some of my sympathy for the mole disappears when I feel he almost enjoys the power he holds over adults. We all give our passports... The situation is both a routine and deadly serious. The other two soldier-kids are walking around the vehicle.

The next few seconds pass. The soldier looks in the passports, a little longer in mine. He looks up to compare my face to the photograph. Up to this point, no words had been exchanged; the oft-repeated gestures were enough, a glance commanding for proof of identity,

intimidating facial movements etc. Suddenly a young voice coming out of a mouth next to a big mole says, in a strong accent, "Are you Jackie Chan?" Without looking at my companions, who had shrunk to the size of children, I said, "yes," punctuating my response with half a question mark, just in case.
He smiled, said something to the other two and let us go through.

I watched an interview with Jackie Chan during which he explained that many people call him "Jackie Chan" on the street. And he said, "Well, I love it, because I know I'm famous, but I don't like when they make the international hand gesture of kung-fu."

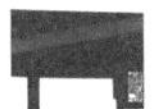

At the end of my stay, I had a taxi booked for Ben Gurion airport. I somehow wished I could meet my geography teacher again. The evening before my flight, my hosts had warned me for the potential difficulties of getting my plane. I am not an anxious flyer, but I listened to the fact I should be there in advance. Five hours early, which seemed overly cautious, I just nodded and prepared myself. The rest of the evening is blurry as one can easily find alcohol in Ramallah and good company to keep you from returning to the hotel at a reasonable hour. I remember the good times and meeting two filmmakers, one Palestinian and the other from Kosovo. I joked at the rather peculiar set of nationals we were, including an Iranian curator.

I waited in the lobby of my hotel, hungover and puzzling at the digital billboard facing the hotel. The advertisements were not visible from either side of the road, and I concluded they were aimed at the hotel guests, a giant screen on the other side of the street from the breakfast room. Because of the traffic and the double-glazed windows, it was silent despite the rapidly changing colours of fast-paced adverts for soda, concerts and other products. I didn't feel like being part of the target audience. My hosts had booked a taxi that was not from Ramallah as it was safer to avoid mentioning I had been in Palestine. A taxi in a different colour pattern than the ones I got used to seeing stopped. The driver hailed me. I don't speak Arabic but he understood English. He says, with a worried and grave face: "Don't worry," which changed my status from relaxed to worried. I had not done anything, so everything should be fine, but he repeats, detaching the words: "Don't. Worry," which now sounds like I should start to worry. The second thing he says is, "you have been to Jerusalem?" And I said, "Well, no, I did want to, but on the very day it was planned, an incident happened, and the situation escalated..."

I unnecessarily explained. "No, I didn't." I quickly rephrased. He doesn't listen to my answer so much and quips, "Don't say you were in Jerusalem." I got confused. His following instructions were increasingly perplexing. He put his hand on my shoulder and told me to state at the airport that I had stayed at Hotel Royal. I turned around to check the hotel sign: Hotel Royal. I stayed at Hotel Royal the whole time in Ramallah. "Is there a problem with...?" But he didn't answer any of my questions, so I got very anxious while he was also sweating on this very early and chilly morning. It would have been very comical if it wasn't for the fact this adult man was visibly scared. To recap, I had to state that I had not been to Jerusalem or stayed at Hotel Royal, which should be easy to remember because it was true.

It was still dark when we left Ramallah, and the drive had a cinematic quality. I could almost hear a soundtrack and see myself looking out the window, trying to focus on the landscape, the people going to work, the building – anything but what might happen at the airport. As a French citizen it isn't easy to understand how borders are anything but a formality. I remember being fascinated by my parents' Japanese passports, which clearly stated the document granted authority to travel anywhere in the world EXCEPT North Korea. With a French passport, one would need a visa, which is more or less challenging to obtain but not impossible. My thoughts were occupied with occupied territories, ancient and recent history and politics, my inadequate knowledge of the situation, and my friends from both so-called sides. I wondered if my very close friend Yaïr would ever meet my very good friend Noura. As my mind was preoccupied with friendship, I was peeling and eating a grapefruit, shoving the skin in my pocket.

It takes a little more than an hour to start

seeing motorway signs for the airport. The sun appears and heats up the morning. The taxi driver had been silent the whole way. When the airport control tower appears, he turned around, to offer an unconvincing smile. Our car is stopped in a long queue of vehicles. Half go through, others are invited to another lane toward a checkpoint. Soldiers with guns inspect the vehicles, and we are told to get out of the car. I stretch, pretending this is routine for me. An officer approaches; he is shorter than me but twice the width with bulging biceps, a polo shirt a size too small. He sports a pistol holster like in cop shows from the seventies. It looks good and impressive. He is pretty young; again, this is disproportionate to the power, the gun, muscle, and testosterone; his English is rudimentary, my Hebrew nonexistent.

"Where are you from?" he asks, looking left and right, already tired this early in the morning.

"London."

He looks up and tries to hide how his preconceptions are shaken.

"London?" he checks if he heard it right.

"Well, I'am French." I quickly add.

"Passport," he commands; something was bothering him.

"Come," he orders and I follow into the barrack.

I sometimes use the shortcut of saying, I'm from Tokyo, which is not true, but I know that some people... I can get rid of them quickly by saying that. I considered the option, but I went for the truth, however suspicious it sounds.

I have his full attention now. He looks in the passport, then at me, the passport again, holds it so as to compare picture and reality, adjust the distance for the ID photograph to be at the same size, closes one eye, kills a chuckle, scratches the corners of the photo, carefully reads the info, checks again with reality by looking at me while I am standing still—this time I smile trying to recapture the photographic awkwardness, reflecting on the best way to look harmless and subservient— scans the passport, his eyebrows wave a couple of times, looks at the old computer screen, eyes reflecting an average information page, goes back to the official document, is annoyed at the plastic cover and takes it out, a few pieces of paper, which I purposefully inserted fall: a drawing of my daughter, emulating the father he could be, a small Post-it Note with a red heart drawn on it by artist Flavia Muller-Meideros who once told me she likes to see the reaction of customs officers when they get to the page, a business card of professorship in an Art school in Geneva (surely this counts although he needs not knowing it was made after I was fired), takes a loupe and checks small prints, shows his colleague the passport, colleague who cannot hide his surprise and looks at me to gauge reality, etc. The situation is far from comfortable but pretty standard in my experience of crossing borders. In this instance, I know this control is already longer than any I have witnessed from the taxi in the last half hour. Despite the similar circumstances, this is a little different because I sense he is not a foot soldier/clerk but a higher ranking officer, the way his equally frightening minions look at him. He doesn't even bother trying to keep a polite surface. It starts to look like a French police movie from the eighties, but I mostly acknowledge my ignorance of the situation. What, me, worry?

I glance outside. The taxi driver is also being interrogated. I am crossing fingers in my pocket we have the same answers. I feel the wet grapefruit skins. As I spot and go toward a bin, a soldier follows me and checks what I am about to throw away.

The difference between landing and taking off from here seems to be that at Ben Gurion Airport, they don't ask you whether you come to Israel or Palestine. They also don't check your luggage content if you are not on a specific list. On the way out, it suddenly matters what your suitcase contains and if you've been to Palestine.

My suitcase is beautiful. Aluminium. A costly object that is both strong and light. You can also see it in classic movies from the fifties and sixties. It goes well with the shiny fuselage of silver airplanes one can picture dangerously passing the top of snowy mountain ranges in the Andes, blue sky and the sun reflecting its wings. This suitcase means "travel". It is ridiculously expensive, by far the most costly item I am traveling with. Its wheels are slightly blocked at an angle that makes it painful to push around. This beautiful suitcase goes through a scanner. Having scrutinised hundreds of customs officers looking at a double screen, changing x-ray colours to detect metal or else, I'd say most are bored and, at best, present a casual attitude towards their task. They are used to water bottles exceeding the allowed limits that were forgotten despite numerous signs, the massive tubs of cream one couldn't possibly consume in less than a couple of semesters packed for a week-long holiday. There is never anything special I have ever witnessed. Is it because the possibility of a terrorist hiding a weapon in a hand-luggage is now low? This customs officer was different. He had an intense paranoid look—or was it how they should all look like?—checking for the longest time anything appearing on his screen, pointing at details, asking colleagues about it. I imagined small bits of geometrical shapes, which, if assembled, would become a handgun, the stuff of spy movies.

My aluminium suitcase goes in. I didn't expect them to scan luggage that would be checked in. I am not worried about the Swiss army knife, but from the facial expression of the now agitated scanning agent, his job purpose finally made sense in this very instant. I could swear he smirked, looking at me. "Gotcha" is what I hear him think before he calls all his colleagues, all armed.

Two of them carry the suitcase to a searching desk in front of me, and as they open it without asking, one barks: "What is your job?"

It shouldn't be but it is a tricky question because depending on who is asking, I tend to change my answers. For example, if you apply for an art residency, it is generally better to say you are an artist than to say you are a graphic designer. If you want to get a grant for an exhibition project, maybe say curator and if you want to get some money for a publication, you'll be a publisher. I am not a professional of any of those; I have usurped the title a few times and gotten away with it. When I meet what I call a "slash person", someone wearing many hats, Jack of all trades etc. and expressing it, I am annoyed but I am guilty and embarrassed of being one. However, I'll try to avoid slashing, such as introducing myself as a designer/artist/publisher/writer/performer/educator/

chef/travel enthusiast, none of which I am terribly good at for lack of the necessary time to perfect any of them. The only one I have a diploma for, which I have never had to show or use, is the graphic designer hat. Your job description is not your ©v but accordingly to a situation I have used the looseness of what I think is someone's perception of each job, in essence. I don't think I am lying because I have taken each role, albeit mostly out of my depth.

This was precisely the moment when you shouldn't be too loose. I answered the customs officer's question about my job as a graphic designer. It's a real job, and I have noticed it is the one that intrigues people the least. They move on quickly. I once was sitting at a workshop, and everyone was introducing themselves. The woman to my right was very excited by this group, she was commenting a lot to the people whose practice she "felt very much close to". She explained at length she was a radical performer. There was a lot of bragging to my taste and I wasn't quite enticed to spend a whole day with her. When she added she was vegan but sometimes ate meat, I couldn't resist commenting she was an "occasional vegan", and a few people chuckled. She attempted to kill me with her gaze. It was my turn to introduce myself. Learning from what just happened I omitted most of my hats even if multiplying job descriptions could open other people's interest. It could also make eyes roll. I introduced myself as a graphic designer, to which she visibly reacted as uninterested and didn't speak to me for the whole duration of the workshop. For her, and quite frankly for most people, being a graphic designer doesn't bring any questions, and if you want to move on, I recommend using that one.

At the airport, I believed that stating being a graphic designer would be both tedious and serious enough for them to let me go and catch my plane.

hey were, on the contrary, visibly
happy my answer didn't match with what
they had seen in my case, which now lay
open for all of us to see as evidence.
It is mostly blue foam with little
compartments; my underwear or clothes
fit in the corners and edges, essentially
padding the foam padding. Each
compartment snuggles a body part.
A leg
another leg
an arm
another arm
a head
eyes
a chest
breasts
hips
a heart
a liver
a lung
a spleen
As they opened the suitcase upside down,
body parts fell in slow motion. Fatima fell

out of the suitcase, piece by piece, the officer with his white gloves tried to prevent them from breaking, but some parts did. The heart resisted.

This is Fatima. Fatima has an arm, Fatima has another arm, Fatima has a chest, she has breasts, a heart, eyes, she has a face, a head, and she has a leg, another leg, hips...

Three faces turn to me, and one mouth asks: "What is this?" I am a cooperative citizen of the world. I have personal opinions about the conflict here in this particular region of the Middle east, but I understand this is unrelated to the content of my luggage. I agree with it being a relevant question, so I comply and am about to answer when it strikes me. I am not sure I know the answer. Why am I travelling with Fatima? I have for a few years, and the normality of it superseded an original reason I have not entirely moved from an intuition that she was to travel.

"Officer, this is a good question," is not

what I say but think.

"Officers—seven of them are now my audience, some with unapproving hands on their hips— this is her story," is what I continue thinking.

"She is called Fatima." is what I say.

Telling them it is a sculpture could have been easier. Art gets away with a lot but in this instance I wanted to know myself why it was essential to travel with body parts and, as we'll see later, many unnecessary items. When I teach, I forbid my students to use the "Art" card. If they are working in a public space, they are not allowed to justify their actions by saying they are Art students doing an Art project for an Art college, or at least I try to enforce it.

"Fatima was born in Portugal, in the town of Fátima. A long time ago, in the early twentieth century, three shepherds saw the Virgin Mary just before the end of the first world war. The Virgin Mary, who was very blonde, appeared to two girls and one

boy, approximately ten years old, with their flocks in the middle of nowhere. The Virgin Mary told them three secrets. For some reason, only one of the children could converse with the mother of Jesus. Another could see and hear; the last could only see. The divine apparition happened a few times, and legend goes many of the villagers joined for the final apparition. They all could see but not hear.
In the meantime, the church got involved. At first, they did not believe the children. Two of them got sick from the Spanish flu and died. Lúcia, the last shepherd, became a nun and lived until 2005. She had time to write down the three secrets. I think they are now canonised, and the Vatican has since recognised the events," I say.

Fast forward to today: Fátima is no longer a village but a town where pilgrims come from all over the world. A colossal stadium size cathedral was built where the kids spoke to the virgin Mary.

"Are you religious?" asks the customs officer.

"Well, no, but we, I—suddenly remembering I use "we" as being part of a collective—am interested in what belief does, and I'll confess I have seen or witnessed a couple of events my scientific mind could not quite make sense of."

At the time of meeting Fatima, we were working in Lisbon for a design biennial called Experimenta. Having spent a month in residency in the capital and discussing with new friends, someone mentioned Fátima as a fascinating place. We jumped on a bus and knew it was a good choice when we passed pilgrims walking on their knees toward the holy place.

It was low season, but religious tourists still filled the buses from Lisbon. It was challenging to imagine the landscape where Mary had appeared because of the tarmac, the concrete, the marble and the lack of nature in the place today. On a large marble piazza two older women were walking towards one church on their knees, wearing kneepads while praying. Their perfect facial expressions of pain seemed genuine enough, transported by metaphysical turmoil yet aware of their physical limitations. Others were throwing white objects into what appeared to be big metal ovens with crosses at their tops. As we approached the people primarily dressed in black, we saw a melting face in the fire. A man threw in an arm and started mumbling a prayer. Other life-size replicas of body parts melted in all the ovens in the area.

These offerings to the fire recalled pagan rituals more than anything I'd seen in a church or even Lourdes. In Mexico, little metal representations of legs or hands could be purchased as ex-votos, a reminder that Jesus had cured or could help cure one disease or another.
We walked towards a busy area; the shops were aligned to serve the pilgrims. We

were hoping for old souvenirs rather than cheaply made plastic snowballs.
In the shops, you can buy flip-flops, candles, keyrings, fans, mugs, and a whole range of nondescript memorabilia; one can even stamp a logo or an image on it. The heat-sensitive mug with the Virgin Mary appearing or disappearing was tempting as well as the suffering-but-not-too-much-knee-pads, but what we saw next we had never encountered in the many souvenir shops we had visited in the past: full shelves of body parts wax replicas, armful loads of arms, not just the right but also the left, hands, also right and left, chests of chests, heaps of hips and more. A face here, some eyes there, the pancreas or liver, even a dog. Some parts were difficult to recognise. Was that a knee? Are you suffering from your knee? Then buy the knee. Then you can burn it and pray for your knee to improve. Or you can kneel and pray for your friend's knee.
The prayer and the possible cure are

one thing, but we were more interested in what happens to the body part, its journey from the shop, and being selected and bought by someone. It is now being given a body part soul as it is no longer generic but has become someone's specific knee with its physical failure and pain; it becomes the receptacle of this pain and is infected. The knee goes into the oven and melts. More prayers connect the wax knee to a real knee and the wax is collected at the bottom, minus some having disappeared into the ether of our breathable space. The wax is collected, and the knee is then reshaped into a chest, face, or perhaps another knee. The new knee is carefully displayed on a shelf in the shop. A perfect circle of burning and being reborn if you have a positive mind. It could also be similar to what one can imagine hell to be, an endless cycle of fire. The whole process happens again and again in the town, so the knee never entirely leaves the town of Fatima.

We started to think of this entity "Fatima" who, like most of us, has a head, a neck, a chest, arms, a belly, hips, etc. She is condemned to be born and die in the same place again and again. It was time to take her on a journey and modestly teach her that life is not just being thrown into the fire. Moreover, Fatima only knew one religion, and there are many more, not to mention the beliefs that one doesn't believe. She had to go on a sabbatical.

We could take her to other places, and she would learn about them simultaneously as we did. We were lucky enough that our job mostly involved people knowing more than we did. She would learn about other political views, she would learn about typography, she would learn about food, about dancing, she would learn ethics, etc., very much as we were ourselves learning about such things.
We bought all the body parts we could afford and got her back to Lisbon first, London

second. We purchased suitably robust and very light luggage that would become her plane/train/bus seat, and for years, she has accompanied us.

Fatima never said much, and as it probably is the case with one's children, she follows, and we hope she enjoys the ride.
In our case, Fatima's presence started to disrupt our encounters with other people, whether for interviews or more informal meetings. There is the ritual of taking her out of the suitcase, the unnerving check of whether she has suffered an injury during the trip. She would be set up, usually lying down on a table. Our host would help make space for the extra guest they would never know about in advance.
Fatima constantly changed the actual encounter, especially with a first meeting. And this is why, Mr. Officer, we are traveling with Fatima, and even if we don't define ourselves as religious, we believe faith is part of our life.

Unphased, the officer asked again: "What is your job?"

I don't think this was a trap, possibly an interrogation strategy, to ask the same question and then to check whether someone is lying or wildly improvising. He remembered that I was a graphic designer. Perhaps the underlying question is what this has to do with my profession.

The seven people in the room were right to ask the question. I felt thankful for a B and A that no post artist talk sessions had offered.

"Where are you from?"

I am rolling my eyes mentally, but before I repress an exhaled answer, possibly hinting at exasperation, something stops me. I am a French national of Japanese origin who lives in the UK and am obviously returning home, but for once I didn't fly directly from London. An unusual behaviour. Will this complicate matters? There is a perfectly logical reason why I spent a week in Pristina, Kosovo, just before boarding a plane to Ben Gurion but I remembered I drank the whole evening with a filmmaker from Kosovo yesterday. The coincidence was funny in the bar; how will this play in a police officer's inquisitive mind? As he is holding my passport, I imagine his connection to the central computer telling him I was in Kosovo before this trip. Why? "Why were you in Kosovo?"

A few months ago, when the trip to Ramallah was already pencilled into my calendar, I received an email from Bardhi Haliti. His name was familiar, so my preconceptions were relatively positive. He was inviting our collective to come and talk at REDO, a conference. The dates were set. As this was too close to my Palestinian trip, I answered at length why another edition would be more convenient, etc. As I was about to send the reply, the name "Pristina" suddenly popped up from the memory of quickly scanning the invitation, and I had to verify my geography. Pristina is the capital of Kosovo and, more selfishly, a place I had not visited before. This information alone postponed the email, and as I googled the place, I was taken aback by an architectural oddity representing Pristina according to the internet: its national library.

Being responsible for an unreasonable carbon footprint because of flying too often, I shook my head and hoped Bardhi would invite me the following year.

His answer was immediate, within ten minutes. His tone was amicable, and I believed his promise of treating me well, whatever this meant. Would I reconsider? Quite frankly, he had me at the mention of a country I had not visited, but I felt both burden and guilt. Cursed with pathological difficulties in saying no, I proposed a challenge he could not respond favourably to: "If I can sleep in the national library, I'll come!" possibly punctuated by an embarrassing "lol". For all his youth Bardhi is, as I will learn later, a very well-connected person due to his charisma, persistence, and ability to make things such as sleeping in the national library of Kosovo possible. The next day I received an email. It was a done deal.

Kosovo's recent history is too complex for me to discuss in a Tel Aviv airport. Besides, I am too ignorant and the people I met there would rather move on from the wars and ethnic hate. I learned how the national library's domes were compared to traditional felt Albanian hats and caused controversy. I bought one of those hats for Fatima, and it was there in my suitcase, next to her head.

As promised, Bardhi made it possible for me to sleep in the library. Fatima slept there as well, in the conference room. It was a first for her and a first for me.

Fatima slept well but I walked around as long as my iPhone flashlight would allow. I filmed on my GoPro and it recorded me talking to myself. This was terrifying.

The reading rooms were empty as most books had been burned during the war. The basement held some. Nothing has been done with the film of empty corridors, and noises I am not sure I imagined. It wasn't comfortable but what did I expect? "There were no books, Mr officer. A library with no books." I was now taken to another interrogation room. I hoped this part of my story explained the presence of a white felt hat. They moved on to another item without hinting at the degree of satisfaction I provided.

"What is this brick?"
I'm a collector of bricks. When I go to places, I like to find a brick. It gives a direction to my perambulations. It is a souvenir, I laughed.

"Isn't that a heavy souvenir?"
"It's an excellent question. And your colleagues asked excellent questions, too." I have to think about it, why do I do this? Food for thought. Unfortunately, I was

expected to respond immediately when it did trigger important issues manifested in objects I could probably do without for an easier trip. I was pushed to answer too quickly and resorted to banal clichés. "Well, you know, a brick is an element of construction and participates in societal progress, but at the same time, when it's on its own, it can be a weapon." This was cheesy stuff but also, as the word came out, I tried to drown it and minimise it as a metaphor. I didn't want to say "weapon" while being interrogated at an airport. "It's about construction and destruction." More cheesy stuff. "It's about democracy and anarchy, Mr Officer." I segued about Carl Andre's sculpture from 1966, "Equivalent VII" a minimalist and important artwork, 120 firing bricks, put together... The tabloids went ballistic in the sixties when Tate bought the work. I spoke of the nature of Art, the eye of the beholder. I was talking faster and faster, going away from the brick as a weapon, confessing love for Art – somehow, I was thrilled to open my heart to this guy. So I told him, I'm not really into graffiti, but what I do is, when I see some bricks on the street, I do my kind of graffiti, and I remake a Carl Andre. So, is it vandalism, Mr Officer? I asked and immediately spoke of the 30 or so bricks I had brought back from as many countries to make what, a tiny ridiculous house, I tentatively joked. Come to think of it, all the officers were very patient, letting me digress as much as I wanted. By then I had forgotten my plane or rather, trying to figure out the content of my suitcase became more important to me than being on time. They were helping me.

"It is heavy to transport. The last time I moved house, my friends were not very supportive of the fact that I was collecting bricks." I added, hoping for a laugh that didn't manifest.

Digging into my brain, I was ready to explore why I started such a collection. The officer had unfortunately moved on and was now holding a concrete tile in his hand. "And this?" he asked.

"It is a concrete tile made in Palestine. I was told there are only four workshops left, and each tile is made by hand. I was lucky to visit one a few days ago, where Ahmed showed me how it is made. The trip itself was eerie as in the evening the dust from the road produced fog in the heavy traffic. The darkness was underlined by the wall on our right, the tall concrete demarcation, and its turrets. The driver, silent, and I, resisting the temptation to film, suddenly saddened. The fog followed me on foot as I entered the empty workshop. A single neon light illuminated the space, and everything was covered in a thin layer of concrete. Ahmed was also covered in dust and appeared silently.
I shook hands with the taciturn yet friendly craftsman, who immediately showed me some metal jigs and forms. I recognised the

patterns on the tiles that were piling around us. The process is one of pressure, and a heavy-duty compressor is the main machine. Ahmed mixed several pots of cement with ink and produced a complex pattern in metal he set into a square mould which I measure by eye to be 20cm by 20cm, noting it fitted European standards. I was already planning to buy some to bring back. Ahmed laid a few layers of sand and cement in the shape before he poured the different coloured types of cement into the metal jig's separate compartments. In a quick gesture he mastered, he pulled it out before it set. I like seeing people with better skills than I have, which is most people. After Ahmed finished the tile I asked him if I could make one… I poured gradients of colours to see what happens. Ahmed let me do it but he was shaking his head. "I know this is not how you're supposed to do but do you think it can be a product that people want to buy?" I asked. He said, "But it takes more time to do it." He let me keep the wrong tile. My attitude of the curious idiot had become a habit, a method.

"I wonder what he thought, Mr Officer. You might wonder why it is wet. Those tiles need to be plunged into the water for 12 hours to solidify. This is what I did as soon as I went back to the hotel after the workshop, and just before going out for the last time in Ramallah. I realised the bathtub or the sink didn't have plugs. I assume that water is too precious to waste for baths. I left the tile soaking in the sink which I filled using a plastic bag. I almost forgot it in the morning"

"Is this a toy?" a new officer asked.
A new team of customs officers had now pulled out a resin figure.
"No it's Jeremy Bentham. Jeremy is a friend of Fatima. Jeremy travels with Fatima. He was an important philosopher and he invented the word "international", Officer. We are at an airport which is international. Don't you think it's amazing?

He also invented the panopticon prison, and so many more things... The original Jeremy Bentham, you can meet in person at University College London. He is the inventor of the auto-icon. Jeremy was aware of his importance and instead of having a bronze statue made, once you're dead, he thought you could be taken to a taxidermist where they stuff you and they make a statue of you, not in a different material such as bronze but in you as material. It's like a mummy but with the intention of being public. Fatima and I had just interviewed Nick Booth, a curator at UCL and he told us at lenghth about Jeremy Bentham. I thought Fatima should meet people like Jeremy, who, like her, transcended death.

My dad was in China at the time and he sent me pictures of artisans who can make resin replicas of anyone from photographs. I sent my freshly taken picture of Jeremy and a few weeks later, here he was, ready to come travel with Fatima. And why he is even a friend, Mr Officer, of Fatima, is because I think there is a relation here, don't you think?

"Do you read Arabic?" The customs officer produces a book and a keyring. "I don't, no." I had bought a book because of the way it looks. A pathetic formalist compulsive collector is all I was. I felt stupid. At least I resisted getting a tattoo in Arabic and Hebrew characters, imagine that. The keyring represents the letter T in Arabic but I confess I got it made because it looks like a smiley face to my ignorant and western-centric self. In Ramallah, I saw a sign for a driving school and laughed because it reminded me of a smiley face. Later that day I saw a street craftsman who was carving arabic letters in pieces of wood, little religious pendants. I asked him if it is ok to have the letter T on a round shaped piece of wood? He happily made it. Was it for me a method of telling Fatima how shallow I was, that

80

I cannot read Arabic, and this makes me smile, and... I feel a bit guilty about it. So I said, "Mr Officer, I did feel guilty about it, because sometimes as a graphic designer, I'm drawn toward form, I'm a formalist. I shouldn't be."

"Why were you there?" is a question that would have come earlier if not for the long-winded stories about the objects. And I tell them, "I was doing a job. A visual identity for an Art biennial that happens here, or rather there in Ramallah." A few years back in London, I met this Palestinian artist... when I said it, I thought, well, this won't be in my favour, but I'm not going to lie. "We designed a logo for him and a Palestinian airline company he came up with. The other curator is from Iran, we met in Sweden." Suddenly, everything that I am saying feels very suspicious. It's suspicious for him or them, but it makes me wonder about all these different connections and different countries and it made me happy and also scared at the same time. I can only assume they were talking about different people they knew and we were the common denominator.

The interrogations happened in different offices but eventually I am in the airport and a single interrogator is standing in front of me, my luggage open again between us. She is a young woman with glasses. She is attractive. This is very shallow, but it was a change from the menacing bulky men. I went full blast visual identity preconceptions and I thought, she is quite young, so she must be progressive, more from the political left, and she has glasses, so she must be intelligent.
She asked me all the same questions:
"What do you do?" I was given another chance to answer this question. The objects I was interrogated about did not relate to graphic design, this time I gave everything: designer, artist, publisher, performer, exhibition producer, teacher...

Am I dispersing myself too much or is it all the same job? I gave my whole CV to this person, a CV that I promised to revisit after this. She didn't blink, roll her eyes or show any facial expression but asked or rather, ordered:

"Show me your website." In the airport, there was a free wifi connection. I understood what websites were for. Precisely for this moment, when someone needs to check how professional you are.

When I showed the website I was aware that its look didn't quite cut it for the moment. Why do we want to not show anything? Why is it so difficult to just represent our honest work on a simple and honest website? Is this some kind of pretentious attitude towards representation? Are we overestimating what we do when shown on a website? Does it reveal how mundane the whole thing is? A lot of our friends happily show what they do, it's how you get jobs... there is nothing negative about it.

The officer didn't give up on me, she didn't judge my book by its website, and she didn't say it was ugly or unprofessional. "What did you do in Ramallah?"
Good, this was concrete and recent. "Well, it is visual identity... When you asked me where I was from and I said, London, then Paris and then Japan, and... I said this is interesting, you asked me, and you thought that I was not Japanese, or that I was Japanese... it is sort of about visual identity and this is what I did in Ramallah. What I do is something that also relates to what we are doing here, speaking." This was messy.

"I was invited to design a visual identity for an Art Biennial in Ramallah. Not just a logo but the way it looks visually, the way it wants to look but also peppered with truth, how it is. In theory, it is possible to do this from anywhere in the world, a brain, a computer, and an internet connection. Some people manage to do it. For me it is not only difficult, I am trying to stay away from the computer as much as possible. Travelling is almost an aim. I developed a method that would require people to invite me physically. We did this first in Berlin with Patrick from the collective. We argued that to design an issue of a Berlin-based skateboard magazine, we had to be taking photographs of street signs, shop signs, graffiti, or anything on the street. They were very accommodating. They bought flight tickets, arranged an apartment and we even got two great bikes to move around to do our job. At the time we called it "Typography safari". This was coined by our friend David Poullard, a very good french typographer. The name has connotations so we have since changed it to "TypographyGo". It is a method of creating a typeface with characters found around the commissioner's place. We have done this in Orléans for a Contemporary Dance Centre and now in Ramallah." I was not sure how interesting this was for my interviewer but since they had submitted me to successive interrogations, I was happy to oblige in details they were not necessarily asking for. Perhaps this was similar to some artist talks.

This method allows you to move around and then discover some things by accident. For example, you can discover that a © could be used in the logo of an Arab Bank, even though Palestinians don't have their currencies, which you know… So, the typeface carries information. The best is to wander around with other people, to create this alphabet as a workshop. One participant told me about a paradox that the "P" doesn't exist in Arabic, sorry I paraphrase here and simplify but Palestine should or could be Falestine. I then noticed that the "P" that doesn't exist was on every car number plate: P.

The "w" comes from a sign advertising a mobile phone network. One of the curators later said we should not use it as they are not sponsors of the Biennial.

I am not finished with it, as this selection

of letters is very recent." I explained to the patient officer with glasses.

This event lasted for four hours, it happened in four offices, in front of 17 officers. As artist talks go, it is not a big audience but every single one was very engaged and asked questions. It is rare to be giving talks without shoes or a belt. I had neither a pen nor a sketchbook and my iPhone had been confiscated.

Finally, they let me go, with Fatima who had gained a few scars and stories to tell. I made it to the plane and during the two hours to Istanbul where I'd change my plane to London, I wrote everything that I just told you.

Thank you very much.

Later

I feverishly wrote down the details of my interrogation. The plane went first to Istanbul where I would have to go through customs and wait for another flight to London. Most of the story was written down when we landed at Sabiha Gökçen Airport. I was excited. The events at Ben Gurion had started as a stressful and frustrating experience of abuse but slowly became something entirely different. I was the last one to join a short queue through customs, my mind busy rehashing the questions I was subjected to and the answers I gave, as well as the better answers that were coming to me now. Next time, I thought.
Next time.

I was fast standing in front of the cubicle, I turned around, and the airport on this side looked empty. I handed my passport to the customs officer. He looked at the picture and quickly looked up at me.
"Where are you from?" he asked.
"London," I smiled, ready to go through a routine of retracing my genealogy.
"You look like a musician," he says. He was in his late forties, possibly in his fifties.
"I know, Damo Suzuki, right?" I replied.
He was puzzled and shook his head.
"No, Barış Manço."
I had never heard this name. "Who?"
"You look like Barış Manço. Do you know the singer?"

He invited me into the cubicle and put the music on.

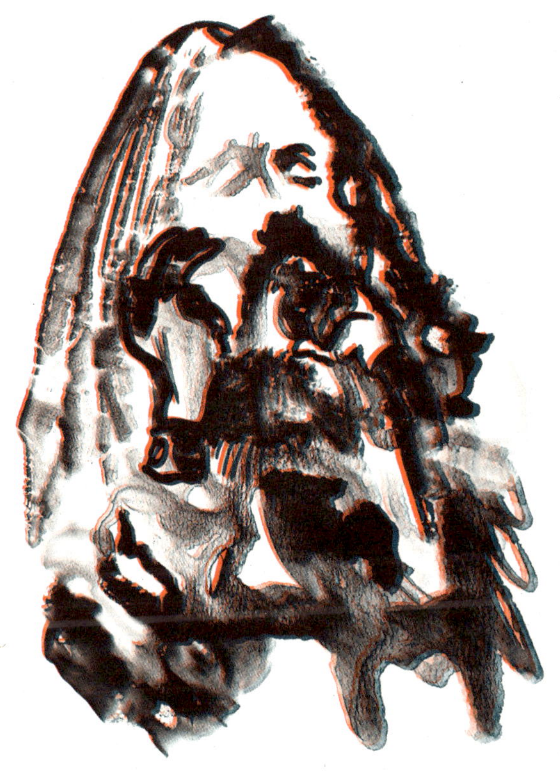

Epilogue

The website abake.fr is no longer active.

The Ramallah Biennial visual identity.
After a few attempts at finishing the job via emails, the visual identity project disappeared and I have not heard from the organisers since.

The Ramallah Brick.
My brick collection was exhibited in *Design is a state of mind* at the Serpentine Gallery, curated by Martino Gamper in 2014. The show toured to Turin and Bolzano. The Ramallah Brick currently lives in London. I still collect them.

The concrete tile was shown in *Vicarious* curated by sandra Doublet at Vivarium in Rennes, 2015, where it was permanently installed in the floor of the artist-run space.

Bardhi Haliti.
I went back to Pristina in 2022 with students from EKA in Tallin. Bardhi still organises REDO and in his introduction mentioned pulling strings for Fatima and me to sleep in the National Library but in his version it took him more than two weeks to get permission.

Fatima.
In 2015, Fatima was invited to tour in the British Art Show 8, curated by Anna Colin and Lydia Yee. She left the suitcase and was assembled by Vincent Humeau and Harry Thaler. She went to Leeds, Edinburgh, Norwich and Southampton. Her belongings, such as the Albanian felt hat, mini figure of Jeremy Bentham and the smiley keyring accompanied her. The keyring was stolen in Norwich. She currently lives in London.

Enter Fatima.

This talk has been presented between 2015 and 2021 in London, Southampton, Leeds, Norwich, Margate, Bolzano, Wadi Rum, Oslo, Edinburgh, Singapore, Brest and Narva.

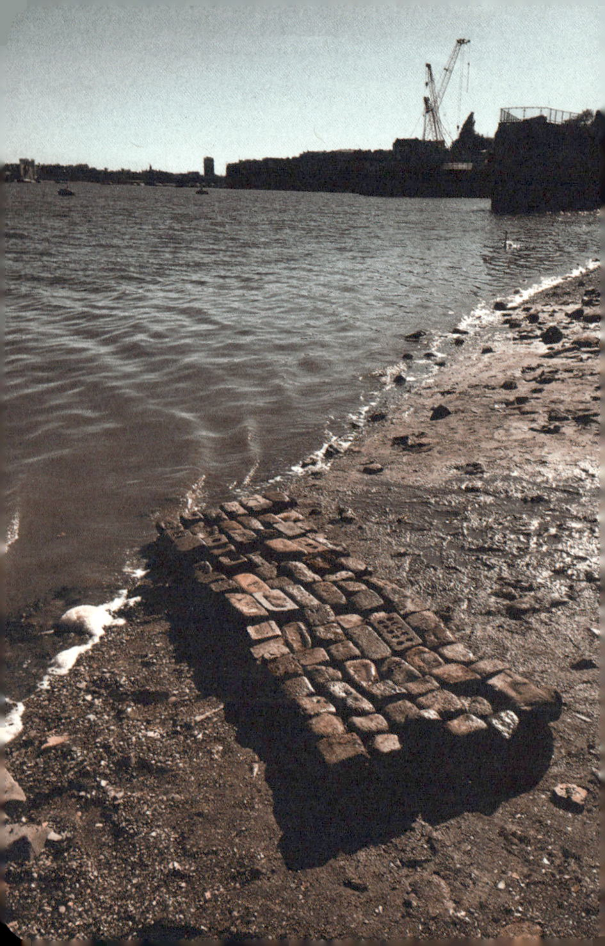

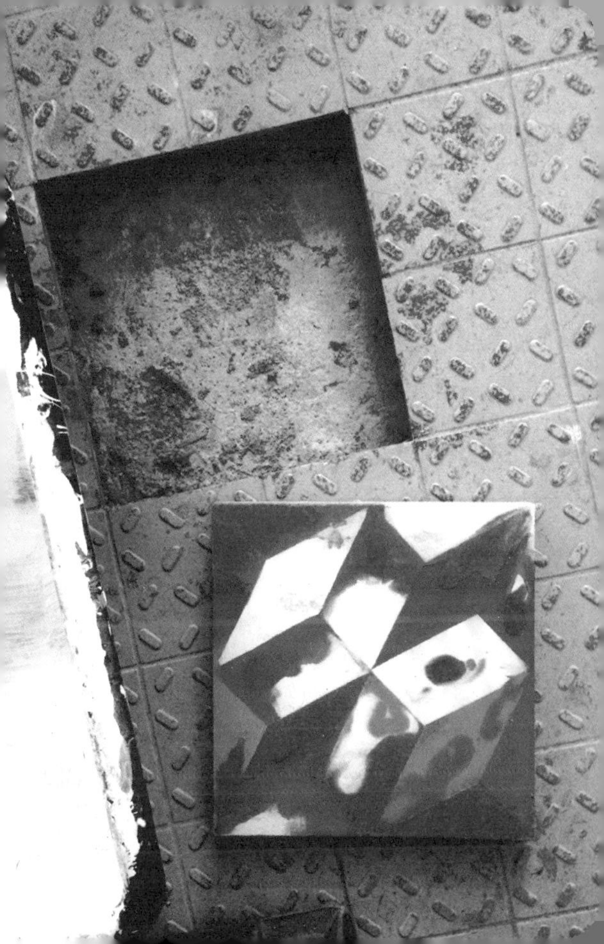

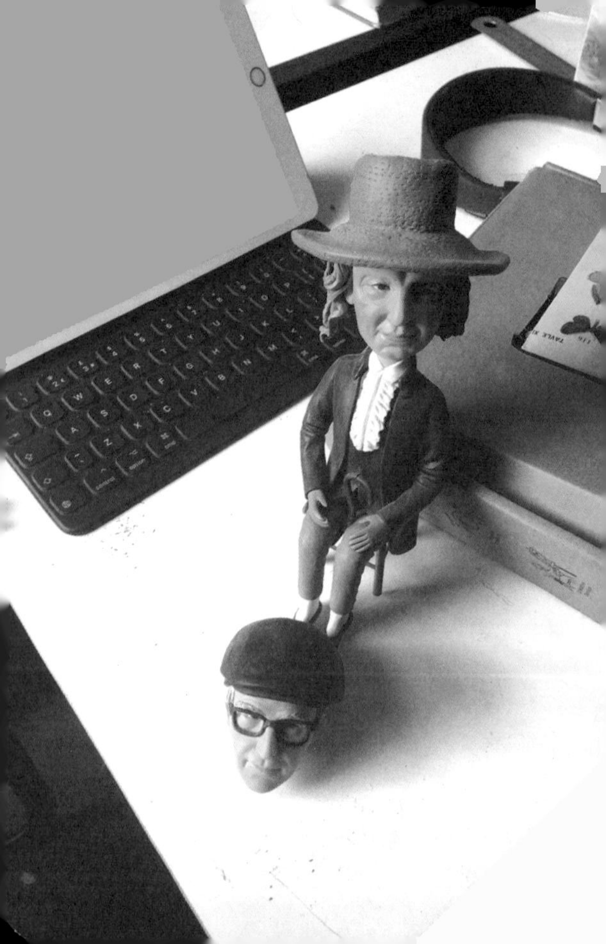

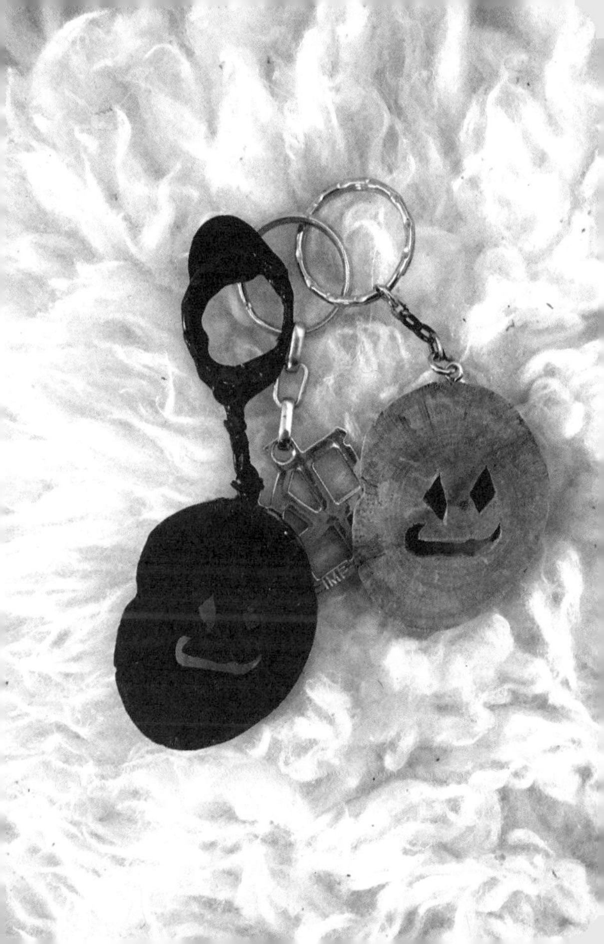

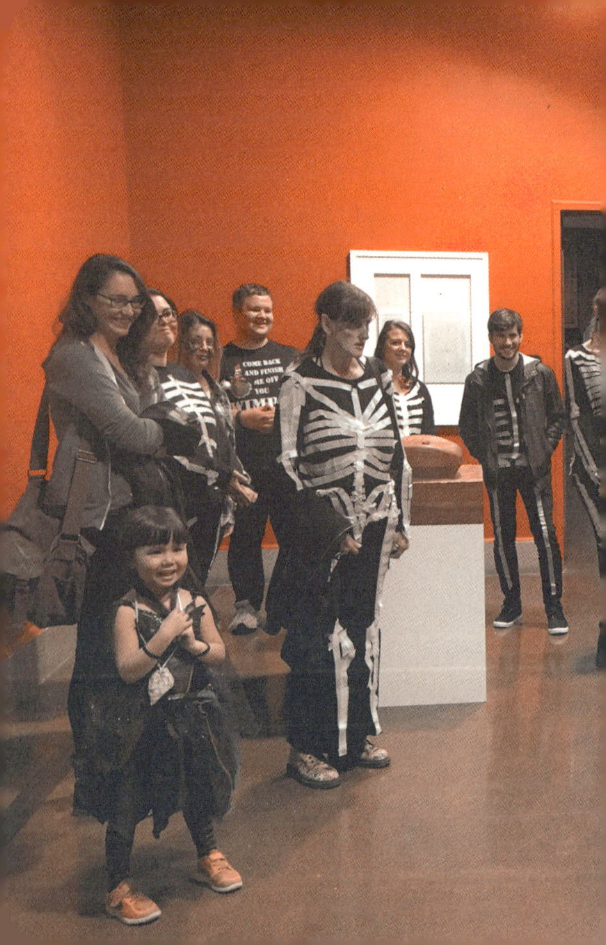

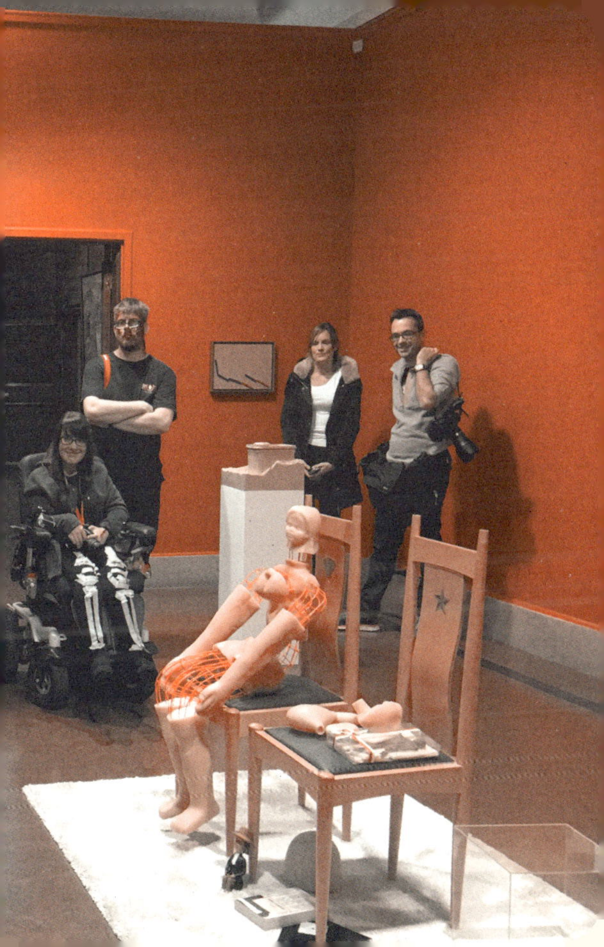

I, Edith

In 2013, åbäke was invited by Loraine Furter to the *Fernand Baudin Students Publications — Dinner/Print Party 23.03.2013 Komplot/Artists Print*, Brussels. Our schedule didn't allow the travel and Loraine proposed we write something that could be read by a performer, a recipe of sorts. She mentioned the performer was called Edith and was aged 25. The following is the text we asked Edith to read/perform.

Dear Edith, thank you for agreeing to read this recipe. We would like you to read the whole text to the audience, including what you just read and anything else including stage directions in brackets for which you are free to change your voice or not.

The text is very conversational and has been written while listening to *Daft Punk Alive 2007*, a concert recording.

[Edith looks at the audience.] I, Edith, have written this text while listening to *Daft Punk Alive 2007*, a concert recorded during their world tour. I was at the concert and I think some of the enthusiastic screams are mine.

[Edith looks at the sheet of A4 on which this is printed.] Hello, My name is Edith and I am 25. I am here to follow the written instructions which I am holding now. As a coincidence, my name is truly, really, actually Edith and I happen to be 25. When I say YOU, I mean you, who are listening to me but also all the yous who will be listening to all the future Ediths who will forever be 25 years old if this is ever performed again, as recipes tend to be. I am also speaking to you who is reading this, both the other Ediths, who will be 25 years old and the people who will be reading this if it is published in printed or electronic form.

[Edith looks at the audience from left to right, smiles if she recognises someone, smiles wider if she wants to meet a stranger, and smiles ambiguously if she thinks you know the person but is not sure from where or when.]

I would like to mention a book I like very much in my kitchen. It is not a recipe book by a TV chef but more of a dictionary or a chemistry book. It has been written by Harold McGee and contains almost no recipes. However, it explains what happens on a molecular level, the chemical implication of, say, a grain of rice thrown into boiling water. Ultimately, it is supposed to help you understand why risotto is risotto. To be perfectly honest I also own celebrity chef books which I sometimes try to hide when foodie friends come to my place.

Oh! this somehow reminds me, well, it is written on this piece of paper that I am supposed to be recalling this memory: my favourite adventure movie is called *My Dinner with*

Andre, directed by Louis Malle starring André Gregory and Shawn Wallace as themselves. I am always a bit confused when actors in a movie play themselves beyond the cameo appearance. Is this to signify it somehow happened even if it is not a documentary reconstruction? Are they playing with my mind? Am I playing with yours? Some of you might have seen it and I do see smiles at my defining of it as an adventure movie. For those who haven't seen it, the whole movie is set in a restaurant. For two hours, two middle-aged men talk to each other. Most of the time it is André who talks. Shawn has not seen him for years and it is about the retelling of the missing years. As a spectator, we only follow the chit-chat of two guys both at least twice my age in a restaurant telling about an adventure that happened a while ago halfway across the planet. I wrote down what they eat while the stories unfold: quail cooked with raisins, rice on the side, then a fish terrine, a potato soup, a salad, an amaretto and a coffee.

I realise now that I am speaking to you in English although Brussels is primarily French-speaking. I will therefore translate what I just said.

Chère Édith, merci d'avoir accepté de jouer cette recette. Nous voudrions que tu lises ce texte devant le public, y compris cette phrase et les didascalies entre crochets. Ce texte très informel a été écrit en écoutant l'album de Daft Punk intitulé *Alive 2007*, qui est un enregistrement d'un concert.

[Édith regarde le public et dit] C'est moi, Édith, qui ai écrit ce texte en écoutant *Daft Punk Alive 2007*, un enregistrement d'un concert auquel j'ai assisté. Je m'entends crier à peu près au milieu du disque.

[Édith regarde la feuille A4 et dit] Bonjour, Je m'appelle Édith et j'ai 25 ans. Je suis ici pour lire les instructions qui me sont données sur cette feuille. La coïncidence fait que je m'appelle réellement, vraiment, Édith et que j'ai 25 ans. Quand je dis VOUS, je m'adresse à vous, qui êtes devant moi, mais aussi aux futures Édith, qui auront toujours 25 ans, les gens qui l'écouteront lire ce texte et aussi ceux et celles qui pourraient lire ce texte s'il est publié.

J'aimerais vous raconter une histoire qui me fait un peu honte, mais je profite de l'occasion pour sauter à l'eau. Il y a quelques années, lorsque j'étais étudiante j'avais pour habitude d'aller dans un café à Bruxelles que beaucoup d'entre vous devez connaître. J'écrivais à l'époque une thèse sur le cinéaste Jean Eustache. C'est un petit café dans une rue très peu fréquentée à Ixelles et les touristes n'y vont jamais. C'était parfait pour être un peu au calme et rester toute la journée en ne consommant qu'un seul café. Le patron était très cool et ne venait jamais en arrière salle. Je fréquentais l'établissement depuis quelques semaines lorsqu'un jour, je me suis aperçue d'un petit manège en observant attentivement le va-et-vient des gens aux toilettes qui se trouvaient au sous-sol. À chaque fois qu'une femme seule y descendait, un homme, pas forcément le même, la suivait. Au départ je ne faisais pas attention, mais j'ai réalisé que tous les hommes de l'arrière salle semblaient se connaître bien qu'ils ne se parlaient jamais. À chaque fois, donc, qu'une femme descendait, il y avait des mouvements furtifs et des échanges silencieux comme pour convenir d'un code ou d'un ordre. C'était très intrigant bien qu'assez effrayant. Les femmes remontaient toutefois assez rapidement donc je ne pouvais pas vraiment penser que des choses terribles se passaient à la cave. Curieuse, je suis quand même descendue et je me suis mise à regarder de très près ces toilettes. Finalement j'ai trouvé un trou dans une des portes qui était presque imperceptible, mais qui n'était certainement pas un accident. Il avait été fait par quelqu'un sans l'ombre d'un doute. J'étais dégoutée et excitée à la fois. J'avais à l'époque un petit ami qui est d'ailleurs dans la salle aujourd'hui avec qui tout se passait très bien et nous étions très amoureux. Malgré cela, ce trou m'a obsédé pendant si longtemps qu'un mois après sa découverte, je décidais de suivre une femme au sous-sol. On ne voyait jamais à quoi elles ressemblaient à cause de la configuration des escaliers. On pouvait deviner l'âge ou si la fille pouvait être jolie, mais on ne voyait pas le visage. Lorsque je trouvais enfin le courage de suivre quelqu'un c'était une blonde un peu ronde avec des Nike et un pantalon noir quelconque. Une fois arrivée en bas, j'ai fait semblant de me laver les mains, mais je finis par regarder dans le trou pour découvrir le sexe de la fille ! Je me suis immédiatement sauvée et je ne suis pas retournée à ce café pendant des semaines. Je n'en avais pas parlé à mon petit ami, car j'avais honte, mais ça me travaillait, car en y repensant, les hommes qui étaient dans ce bar n'avaient pas vraiment le profil ou en tout cas l'idée que je me faisais d'un pervers. Certains d'entre eux étaient plutôt beaux garçons, surtout un qui présentait très bien, si je peux dire, bourgeois intello, qui ressemblait un peu à cet acteur français des années 80, je ne sais pas si vous voyez, Michaël Lonsdale. Après un mois, cependant, je n'ai pas pu résister à y retourner pour observer le manège de ces hommes et de ces femmes.

Voilà, merci.

Dear Anne

The following text was recorded during a presentation in an international typography symposium titled *Lettres Modernes #2 Voir, regarder, lire* (Modern Letters #2 See, look, read)" 27-28th March 2014 in Caen, France.

This symposium was organised in the context of the research activities of ésam Caen/Cherbourg and led by Jean-Baptiste Levée, in partnership with the Arts Graphiques festival of the University of Caen Basse-Normandie (ARG3).

Anne Millet who was not present at the conference transcribed it the week after the intervention. In 2022, it was translated into English by Anna Miles for this publication and performed on a bus in Hungary on the 5th of October 2022.

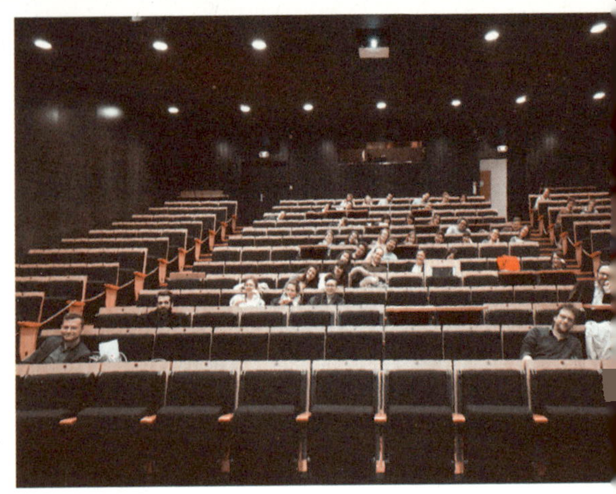

Hello, I say hello to you but also those in front of a screen or printed matter, reading this. But really, I say hello to Anne.

Anne, good morning. It is the 3rd of January 2014. I received an email from Jean-Baptiste Levée, who I vaguely know of. He has invited me to speak at a symposium called "to read, see, speak" or something like that. I saw the list of people invited and they seem pretty serious or at least more legitimate to the subject of this gathering, an international typography symposium, than we are. I'll ask him during my lecture why he invited us amongst otherwise very professional typographers. As you know we are somehow interested in letters so we agreed to participate even if suddenly being amongst real pros could reveal the fraud.

Recently, archaeologists found ancient petroglyphs near Glasgow. The experts can't read them but what is fascinating is their theory it could be some kind of proto-writing. Imagine people who don't know what writing is but will engrave something in stone to try it out for the first time! Jean-Baptiste Levée said this talk would pay 250 euros. To get the petroglyphs tattooed would cost 140 euros and pretty much the same to get them erased afterwards. What do you think? Shall I get this tattoo done? I thought this would be relevant to the talk and the symposium, about ink, writing, typography etc.

Anne, it is 2 am in my crappy hotel room. The TV is still on. I woke up suddenly because of your name. Anne is a homonym of Diane..
We have never met but we have exchanged emails. I asked you to transcribe this talk but I started recording before the talk itself, which I am now telling the audience about. I can't help but think of

this relationship we have created. I am talking to you through the recorder on my phone, sometimes my laptop and sometimes during the talk, which is being recorded by the symposium staff. I imagine you would be at work, in front of a computer, with headphones on, listening to what I am saying, deciphering mumblings and dodgy grammar, and typing it.

I woke up because I thought this is wonderful, that you are like Diane. Do you remember Diane? Have you seen David Lynch's Twin Peaks? I don't know how old you are but from the brief professional emails, I would say you are in your mid-thirties and would assume you have seen this American TV series in which Special FBI agent Dale Cooper constantly spoke to Diane in his recorder during his murder investigation. I always thought Diane to be his assistant, back in the office but what if Diane was the name of his recorder?

Anne, this is the first of March 2014 and I decided to decline the invitation to this conference because I don't have the time, being busy with too many looming deadlines. I'll be honest and perhaps this time reason is a little flaky as I always have time for what I want to do. I just didn't quite understand why it would be interesting for anyone to see our contribution to this symposium. We are perfectly at ease to create typefaces for our projects but it is intimidating to speak before and after actual professionals. I hope Jean-Baptiste will understand my change of heart. It is very soon and it's been announced already. Will he find a replacement at this late hour and, if so, how will the new person feel?

Anne, it is the 2nd of March and I spoke with Jean-Baptiste on the phone. I couldn't say no. I'm not sure how I'll manage as I won't have time to prepare anything.

Third March. Anne, I'm on the train and I can work a little—I hope the background noise won't disturb the transcription. I'm talking and typing on my phone. It is quite small and one can't change the typeface or the size. Is this Helvetica? I'm not even able to recognise a classic. Why am I telling you this?

Anne, it is the 4th of March. I have an idea to structure the talk like an ABC (I was watching Deleuze). I wondered if you could help me. What do you look like? How is your office environment? Do you have specific rituals when you transcribe? What do you do with onomatopoeias? What if I say ghhhhgrrrillllowatsugh? Sorry.

Anne, I was at the National Library and when I went to the toilet I saw this graffiti that said: "thank you if you read this". I first thought it said "F*** you if you read this" which made me chuckle. On closer inspection, it was hand drawn and I recognised the typeface, named Valentine, originally designed for an Olivetti typewriter by Ettore Sottsass. I wondered how this type of letters, made for a very specific Italian typewriter found its way into the National Library toilets, moreover hand drawn to look mechanical. I remembered this typeface had been digitised by the digital foundry Lineto in the early 2000s. There it was, neither printed nor typed.

Anne, it is the 5th of March and I am in Geneva in a generic hotel room. My mood is sombre as I just had a class with some students. One of them showed me a poster he designed. I was intrigued by the choice of fonts and asked why. "Erm, why not?" was his answer. Deep down I couldn't disagree but then what was the point of discussing it at all?

Anne, I have another favour to ask you. In this email containing today's recording, I also attached a typeface I made for you. It is called Anne. I hope you don't find this too strange but I asked the person who recommended you to describe you to me. She mentioned dimples and long hair. I laughed as I have long hair and I know how annoying this simple first detail seems to have consequences on how people perceive me. Anyway, I went along with the physical traits and made this screen font for you with the help of a friend who knows about programming. Please take your time in installing it and now, I would appreciate it if you could type this text on your screen with "Anne". As you see it has this flow, which I thought would be like your hair and the "o" has indents on both sides, like dimples. Pretty cheesy stuff, sorry. I worry I am revealing this is how I design typefaces, on whimsical details. It is only made for the screen. My friend used an algorithm or some kind of bug that prevents the text from being printed from any software. You can't export it either. I'll let you try.

What do you think? It's impressive and scary, isn't it? I'm pretty sure you're thinking that you can screenshot the text but that's the scary bit. We worked with the people who program that sort of technology to prevent scanning banknotes such as US dollars or euros. When you try a screenshot, you'll see an error message! In our typeface, we inserted micro details which are picked up by the actual computer, yours, mine, and everyone's and creates a warning and blocks the command. Same if you try to take a picture of your monitor with your smartphone. I suppose if you had an old analogue camera, it would be possible to photograph your screen. Imagine if you could not, like this flower that refuses to show its colour on camera!

My friend is a tech genius. He's moving to

California to work for . Please don't give this typeface to anyone as we made it for you, for this conference.

Anne, it is the 17th March and the conference is approaching fast. I have not written anything yet.

I was thinking of Star Wars. Did you notice they don't have paper? They have so many meetings and their monitors are rudimentary but they don't have any paper with important documents to sign or file in boxes. They have Jedi meetings with incredibly complex decisions but they never have a piece of paper to write on or to report. Incidentally, the Jedi council doesn't have a table and some of the important characters are sometimes shown behind a desk but there is nothing on the desk. No piles of paper, not a single sheet of A4. A whole universe without paper. What do you think the consequences would be? Are we getting there too?

In my last talks, I noticed people were taking notes on their laptops or at least they seemed to be doing so from where I stood. You are probably typing it on a computer. The only trace it has once been said are the hesitations, "erms", stuttering and embarrassing "You know", "I mean" or "like" that litter my speech.

Anne, 20th March. The typeface named "Anne" which I gave you I thought I could give the people at the conference. I'll see how sympathetic they are and if I am really happy and there is a connection with the audience I'll give them the typeface. Looking at it with fresh eyes, I find formal similarities with a font called Silian Ray. It is elegant if I may say so, round in the mouth, with hints of minerals, a nice colour, and a slight overhang.

Anne, 22nd March, past midnight. I drank too much wonderful Japanese whisky. What is the pangram again? "PORTEZ CE

VIEUX WHISKY AU JUGE BLOND QUI FUME". In English: ZORRO, BRING AND POUR A FILTHY MILD CAVA WHISKEY TO QUENCH THE OBNOXIOUS JUDGE.

Anne, 23rd March. I just finished a website inspired by James Joyce's Ulysses. Did anyone read it? Anne, I am talking to the people in the talk. It is today! Has anyone read it and especially the last chapter? Can you explain what happens there to people who are not familiar with the book?

Voice 1: It's a text with portmanteau words, many of them, it goes all over the place.

Yes, what could you say about the form?

Voice 1: It ends... where it started?

Really? Well, I meant the fact it has no punctuation, following a stream of consciousness. More than 24000 words which, if read continuously, lasts 2 hours, an average length for a movie. We made a website for this chapter, it continuously scrolls right until the final period. I initially thought of making a single paper page but a website seemed appropriate.

Anne, a conference is also called a talk and a lecture. I am talking, you are listening and transcribing. You type something others will read and perhaps I could read it out loud for an audience to hear it. There could be an audio version.

My local library is on Reading Lane.

A friend of mine is called Manuel Raeder but he is not a book.

Many years ago, my dad brought a Chinese bootleg of a Japanese VHS tape of Star Trek. The whole movie is subtitled in Japanese but as a Chinese bootleg, Mandarin and Cantonese horizontal and vertical side titles have been added to the screen. When the Klingons discuss in their fictional language, the English text is added to a now saturated screen. The action itself is very difficult to watch but very well described in four languages. Imagine being fluent in English, Japanese, Mandarin and Cantonese, the impossibility of not reading subtitles, overwhelming the actual image, saturated by others, conjured by words from four different sources.

Anne, it is very noisy, sorry, I am in a karaoké booth and while singing, reading from the monitor, I thought of the typographers in the world who don't have a job. They could work on typefaces for karaoké machines in Japan or Korea. That is a market, perhaps.

Another thought as I am now singing an unfamiliar song. If you don't know the song, the music and its lyrics are not enough,

partly because of silence management.
How does one transcribe silence? For
karaoké, a ping pong ball jumps over the
words to indicate when to sing what or
the sentences change colour according to
the sound. How do you transcribe silence
such as this:

[short silence]

or this:

[longer silence]

The minute of silence in honour of the dead. We could do a minute of silence for more joyous occasions. Let's all do it together. We will be silent for a minute in this talk and you can all think of a happy moment in the past or perhaps imagine a happy moment in the future, ok let's do it. Anne, you do it too, please.

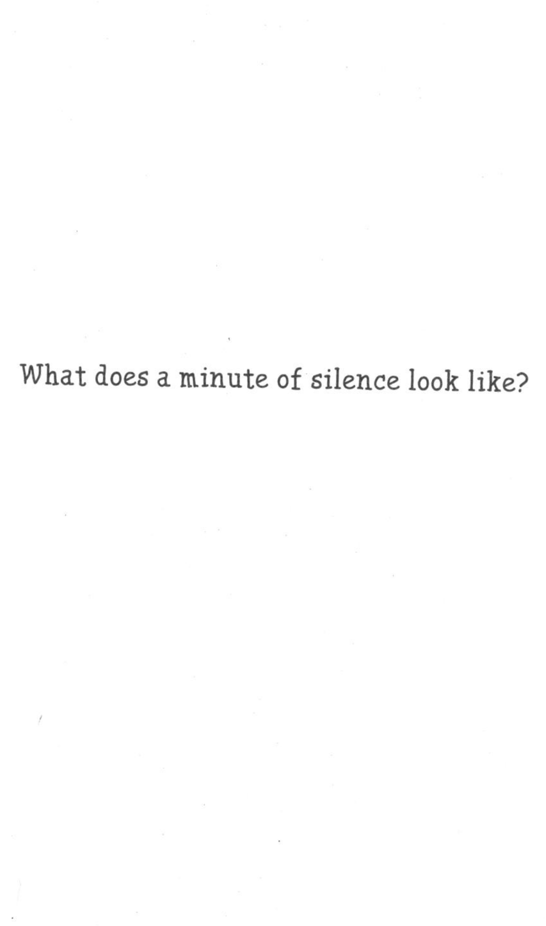

What does a minute of silence look like?

Anne, I will now start the talk. Can you hear the audience arriving? The lecture theatre is quite conventional. The seminar is mostly in French but there are American and Dutch speakers. I notice their absence in my talk. I know some people in the audience. As I already have my microphone on, they can hear everything I am telling you, Anne. They are smiling. We are ready to start. Not full house. Less than yesterday when the Dutch typographer spoke.

I'll ask Sabine to take a picture of the audience. "Sabine, can you take a photo?"

"Oh, yes, sorry, would you mind if I took a picture of you guys? Feel free to hide your face or hide completely if you do mind. You are not a typical audience, atypical, atypographical, sorry this is a bad pun, I'm nervous."

"Ok, let's take this picture. What would be

great is to have a photo in *italics*. everyone slanted to your left. Great, that looks fantastic from here. I feel carried away but now let's take the **bold** version. Can you make yourself **bold**? Right. Thank you, the *italics* picture was better.

Anne, I must do something, give me a minute [muffled sound].

"One, two, three: Happy birthday!
[all sing happy birthday]
Happy birthday to you, happy birthday to you, happy birthday, deeeeeaaaaar Anne, happy birthday to you!"
[applause]

Thank you everyone, thank you Anne!
[applause]

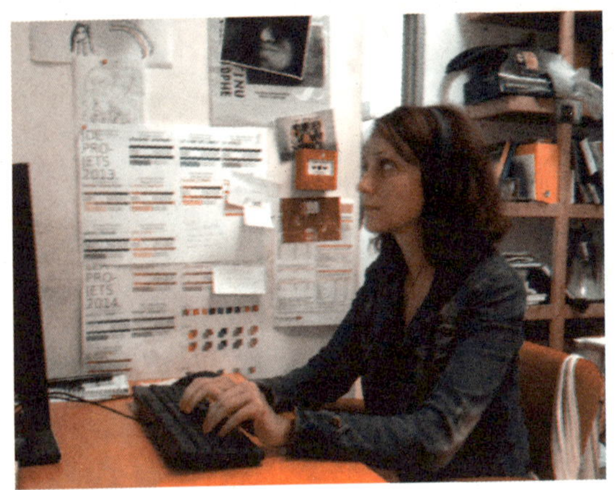

photo: Anne Millet

Amateur Pro

artconnexion invite åbäke & LPPL et Hugo Kostrzewa à créer une performance culinaire au Comptoir Hirondelle à Lille le 19 juin 2022.

Le menu :

Krill Sushi,
Pinocchio la Baleine,
Mammouth d'Amour,
Poutargue de Momie sur Baikal Kombu,
L a i t a n c e In c l u s i fv e ,
Fugu à Mort,
Grande-Mer du Doryphore

Ce qui suit est un courriel du 21 juin 2022 envoyé aux membres d'artconnexion ainsi que les collaborateurices de la performance.

sujet: La performance continuc

En passant la première porte de la gare Lilloise Eurostar en direction de Londres, je souris à la pancarte tenue par un douanier montrant des obus de la Seconde Guerre mondiale dont le commerce et l'utilité en tant que souvenir semblent tellement courants qu'un panneau spécial est nécessaire depuis des années.

J'avais pensé à créer des sculptures en forme de ces choses proscrites à plusieurs reprises afin de provoquer un échange sur le pourquoi. L'évidence de la bêtise d'une telle chose m'en avait empêché sa réalisation. La bêtise, mais aussi la présomption d'un artiste qui prendrait à la légère des mesures qui, si elles paraissent exagérées, existent probablement à la suite de décisions complexes.

Je souris à ce moment récurrent à créer une œuvre avortée dans mon esprit. Une pensée activée uniquement à Lille, Paris, Calais, aux terminaux Eurostar.

Ma valise est conçue spécialement pour transporter un vélo pliable et paraît trop professionnelle, première erreur. À l'examen du scan, son contenu est suffisamment suspect pour une fouille plus approfondie que les douaniers m'ont alors imposé pendant 1h10 dans une arrière-salle sans fenêtre. Trois agent·es armé·es bien que souriant·es et d'une politesse impeccable. L'histoire commence avec un sac rempli de papier mâché encore humide dans le sac à dos. *Qu'est-ce que c'est ?* Me demande-t-iels et je suis autant embêté qu'excité, car ce détritus est une sculpture détruite pour les besoins d'une assurance, récupérée la veille à Anvers et je l'emmène à Londres pour décider de sa résurrection ou plutôt sa réincarnation en une autre chose encore indéfinie. Cet amas est donc post mortem, mais aussi embryonnaire. Les douanier·es sont dubitatif·ves, mais transporter de la poubelle n'est pas forcément illégal.

Nous passons à la valise et mon erreur est d'anticiper l'ouverture par l'annonce que ce sont des sculptures. Ce mot impliquait que les objets avaient été confectionnés, mais iels saisissent l'angle capitaliste et la valeur potentielle de vente. S'ensuit pourtant une discussion courte, mais entendue, des quatre personnes présentes sur la valeur subjective de l'art. Il ne sera donc pas nécessaire de mentionner les excès d'un crâne diamanté ou d'une banane scotchée à un mur, ouf.

Je minimise la valeur marchande des objets en les emmenant vers l'utilitaire de la performance de samedi dernier, ce qui m'autorise à en rejouer des extraits qui captivent au moins deux des douanier·es. L'un connaît le Fugu et explique à sa collègue qu'il s'agit d'un poisson gonflant dont la consommation peut être mortelle. Elle sursaute lorsqu'elle ouvre un papier journal et se voit confrontée à un masque fait en peau de lotte. Je sens les points de sympathie accumulés par le récit descendre en flèche et je jurerais qu'iels vérifient que leur pistolet est bien en ceinture, mais j'exagère sans doute.

La douanière s'empare d'un des objets et elle a une réaction de dégoût à ne pas s'être attendue à ce qu'il soit mou. C'est décidé, iels mettent des gants en latex qui, je les entends dire en aparté entre euxelles, *sentent la beuh depuis que le latex est végétal*. Un moule en latex, un morceau de bois avec des bâtons de réglisse taillés du nez de Pinocchio et tous ces objets que je décris maintenant comme fonctionnels dans une performance avec Hugo et Luna. Fonctionnels donc sans but d'être vendus, mais aussi faits de détritus comme une plaque de terrazzo qui, je l'explique, n'est pas du marbre. *C'est un matériau noble ?* demande la douanière.

Des sculptures certes, mais parfois *ready-made* ou plus précisément *ready-found*.

La barquette, pourtant lavée ayant contenue la laitance de hareng fumé maintenant remplie de coriandre vietnamienne séchée amène un fumet particulier dans cet espace réduit. L'exposition improvisée est saisissante et je prends des notes pour le futur.

Tout devient source de question : mes claquettes en fausses laitues : *c'est quoi ? Des chaussures.* Un papier journal en chinois emballant la coriandre vietnamienne : *vous êtes vietnamien ou japonais ? Français.*

Un manga chinois, cadeau de ma galeriste : *C'est de quand ? Je crois 1984* (pourquoi cette question et pourquoi est-ce que je connais la réponse ?).

L'ormeau éveille tout de suite les soupçons et deux des douaniers se mettent à l'ordinateur pour vérifier qu'il ne s'agit pas d'une espèce protégée. *Combien ça vaut?* me demandent-ils. *Je ne sais pas, ça vient de San Francisco,* et à cette évocation je m'interroge s'ils vont commencer à enquêter sur le transit de l'objet de ces cinq dernières années.

L'un regarde sa montre et dit qu'il est trop tard pour appeler son amie à Tahiti qui saurait peut-être la valeur de l'ormeau. *Il y en a en Bretagne aussi,* dis-je, *c'est délicieux.*

La douanière n'est pas satisfaite des ormeaux googlés qui font 11cm, la moitié du spécimen dans mon sac. Je la vois élargir ses recherches et tombe sur le geoduck, coquillage formidable évoqué par Donna Haraway qui avait été évoqué plusieurs fois dans nos recherches avec Hugo. Je m'abstiens d'élargir les champs d'investigations même si je comprends que mon train est parti et que le prochain sera dans quatre heures donc j'ai désormais le temps.

Iels me demandent même maintenant ce que mes vêtements sont car ils sont utilisés pour emballer des pierres, des baguettes en forme de train à grande vitesse, mais aussi des jeux de cartes pour enfants (j'ai une fille).

Je dois d'ailleurs aller la chercher, je dis, *en espérant humaniser cette situation*, mais en même temps je suis persuadé que cette histoire enchantera Luna, justifiant mon retard à la sortie de l'école.

La révélation d'un plat en forme de mammouth et d'une assiette en morceaux de céramique trouvés dans la Tamise est presque spectaculaire et me permet de parler de Lubya, le mammouth momifié découvert en Sibérie, que le douanier amateur de Fugu connaît aussi.

Vous auriez dû venir à la performance de samedi, je lui dis, sa collègue rajoute : *oui, lui c'est un artiste*.

Tandis que la fouille s'effectue, on me pose plusieurs fois les mêmes questions :

Donc vous avez fait un spectacle à Lille ?

Oui, enfin une performance culinaire.

Dans un théâtre ?

Et bien non, c'était... et j'hésite à dire que c'est un bar et me demande à vitesse d'improvisation s'il est préférable que l'évènement soit plus ou moins officiel et en apparence sérieuse.

Vous avez fait combien de représentation ?

Une seule, malheureusement, mais d'une certaine manière, je vous en ai montré une version courte et je perçois un léger mouvement sur son visage vers l'affirmatif.

Et vous avez été payé combien ? demande-t-elle. Je ne suis pas certain de sa légitimité à poser ce genre de question, mais pour éviter de plomber une ambiance plutôt positive je réponds : *Avec Hugo, 250 euros chacun.*

C'est qui Hugo ?
Jusqu'ici j'avais réussi à ne pas impliquer mon camarade, mais à la longue je me sentais coupable de me créditer seul pour une performance collaborative. Marcher sur ce fil, entre dénoncer un complice et partager des lauriers. Rendre à César ou balancer. J'évite par contre d'évoquer que la collaboration se déroule aussi avec Luna, car elle est mineure.
Hugo est artiste et nous avons travaillé ensemble sur ce projet, il habite Rennes où on peut acheter des ormeaux, d'ailleurs. Soudainement

beaucoup trop d'informations et d'associations rhizomatiques, me dis-je.

La douanière répète cette question que déjà, elle avait posé au premier scan de la valise :

Vous êtes un professionnel ?

Oui, je suis artiste et cette déclaration que, seul, j'avais estimé représenter le sérieux de toustes les travailleur·ses du monde de l'Art (c'est un vrai métier, non ?) a finalement été le déclencheur de cet entretien et fouille systématique.

Je comprends, lorsqu'elle repose cette même question une heure après, qu'elle me donne peut-être une dernière chance d'être un collectionneur-amateur d'excentricités avec une compulsion accumulatrice.

Vous êtes un professionnel et vous n'avez pas d'Athéa ?

Une athéa ?

Un ATA, une attestation qui est un passeport pour le matériel professionnel.

Vite, est-il possible de quitter cette autoroute du professionnalisme en direction du chemin de campagne de l'amateurisme ?

Ces objets ne sont plus des sculptures que l'on pourrait vendre très cher.

Ces objets ne sont plus des sculptures qui sont activées en display lors de performances.

Ces objets ne sont pas des outils professionnels.

Ces objets sont des cadeaux pour des ami·es.

Trop tard.

Ça va vite dans la tête, mais l'atmosphère est calme et je rends les armes, on fait chacun notre métier.

La cheffe douanière se tourne vers moi, presque souriante.

Bon, je ne crois pas qu'il y ait quoi que ce soit que nous allons confisquer commence-t-elle, *mais vous aurez à payer une amende de 150 euros pour avoir transporté du matériel professionnel sans ATA.*

J'encaisse le coup et le coût, partagé entre ma jubilation à raconter l'anecdote et la réalité que je tente de rationaliser.

Ah oui, 150 euros, ça fait beaucoup sur une prestation payée 250, ça rend la pratique presque amateur je lance et ce faisant, me rappelle combien de fois ce rapport à l'argent est une question clé de l'Art, quelque chose de non réglé, un flou entretenu par toustes.

C'est sans rancune et avec une histoire à raconter que je sors de la salle, escorté par Nathalie, Brice et Julien.

PS : artconnexion rembourse généreusement la contravention quelques jours plus tard.

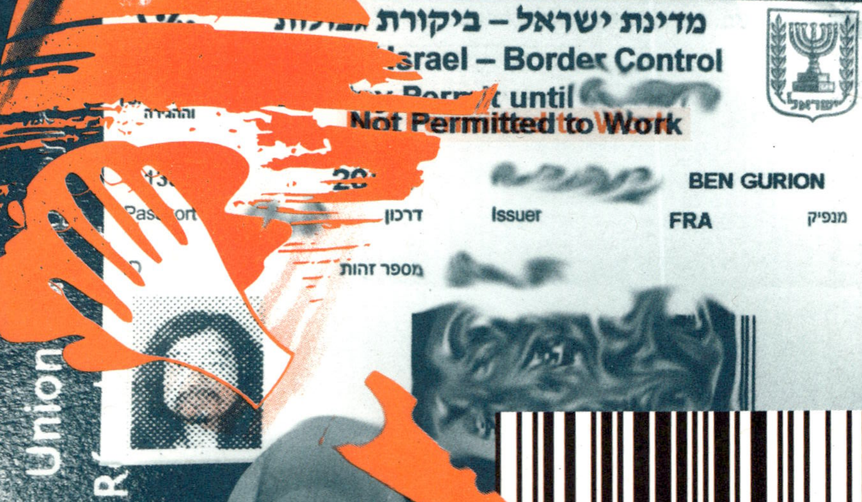
Union
Ref
מדינת ישראל – ביקורת הגבולות
Israel – Border Control
Permit until
Not Permitted to Work
Passport
דרכון
Issuer
מנפיק
FRA
BEN GURION
מספר זהות
ישראל